On Becoming Filipino

Selected Writings of Carlos Bulosan

In the series, *Asian American History and Culture*,
edited by Sucheng Chan and David Palumbo-Liu

Also in the *Asian American History and Culture* series:

Sucheng Chan, ed., *Entry Denied: Exclusion and the Chinese Community in America, 1882–1943*, 1991

Gary Y. Okihiro, *Cane Fires: The Anti-Japanese Movement in Hawaii, 1865–1945*, 1991

Yen Le Espiritu, *Asian American Panethnicity: Bridging Institutions and Identities*, 1992

Karen Isaksen Leonard, *Making Ethnic Choices: California's Punjabi Mexican Americans*, 1992

Shirley Geok-lin Lim and Amy Ling, eds., *Reading the Literatures of Asian America*, 1992

Renqiu Yu, *"To Save China, To Save Ourselves": The Chinese Hand Laundry Alliance of New York*, 1992

Velina Hasu Houston, *The Politics of Life: Four Plays by Asian American Women*, 1993

William Wei, *The Asian American Movement*, 1993

Sucheng Chan, ed., *Hmong Means Free: Life in Laos and America*, 1994

Timothy P. Fong, *The First Suburban Chinatown: The Remaking of Monterey Park, California*, 1994

Chris Friday, *Organizing Asian American Labor: The Pacific Coast Canned Salmon Industry, 1870–1942*, 1994

Paul Ong, Edna Bonacich, and Lucie Cheng, eds., *The New Asian Immigration in Los Angeles and Global Restructuring*, 1994

Carlos Bulosan, *The Cry and the Dedication*, edited and with an introduction by E. San Juan, Jr., in press

Yen Le Espiritu, *Filipino American Lives*, in press

ON BECOMING
Filipino

Selected Writings of
Carlos Bulosan

Edited with an Introduction by

E. San Juan, Jr.

Temple University Press
PHILADELPHIA

Temple University Press, Philadelphia 19122
Copyright © 1995 by Temple University
All rights reserved
Published 1995

♾ The paper used in this book meets the requirements of the
American National Standard for Information Sciences—Permanence of
Paper for Printed Library Materials. ANSI Z39.48 1984

Printed in the United States of America

Text design by Anne O'Donnell

Library of Congress Cataloging-in-Publication Data

Bulosan, Carlos.
    On becoming Filipino : selected writings of Carlos Bulosan /
edited, with an introduction, by E. San Juan, Jr.
        p.   cm.—(Asian American history and culture)
    Includes bibliographical references.
    ISBN 1–56639–309–4 (case).—ISBN 1–56639–310–8 (pbk.)
    1. Filipino Americans—Literary collections. I. San Juan, E.
(Epifanio), 1938– . II. Title. III. Series: Asian American history and culture series.
PR9550.9.B8A6   1995
818'.5209—dc20   94-48937

Contents

Correspondence

Publication History

Stories

"Passage into Life": from the Bulosan collection of the late Dolores Feria (hereafter cited as DF).

"The Story of a Letter": *New Masses* 59 (April 30, 1946): 11–13.

"Be American": *Amerasia Journal* 6.1 (May 1979): 157–63 (hereafter cited as *AAJ*).

"The Soldier": in *Bulosan: An Introduction with Selections*, ed. E. San Juan, Jr. (Manila: National Book Store, 1983), pp. 87–91 (hereafter cited as *Bulosan*).

"As Long As the Grass Shall Grow": *Common Ground* 9:4 (Summer 1949): 38–43.

"Life and Death of a Filipino in America": In *Bulosan*, pp. 25–30.

"Homecoming": in *Bulosan*, pp. 105–111.

"The Thief": in *Bulosan*, pp. 93–95.

"The End of the War": *New Yorker*, September 2, 1944, pp. 21–24.

Essays

"How My Stories Were Written": in E. San Juan, Jr., *Carlos Bulosan and the Imagination of the Class Struggle* (Quezon City: University of the Philippines Press, 1972), pp. 138–43.

"The Growth of Philippine Culture": *Teachers' Journal* 5 (May–June 1951): 1–18.

"My Education": in *AAJ*, pp. 113–20.

"Freedom from Want": *Saturday Evening Post*, March 6, 1943.

"Filipino Writers in a Changing World": *Books Abroad* 16 (July 1942): 252–53.

"I Am Not a Laughing Man": *The Writer* 59 (May 1946): 143–45.

"The Writer As Worker": *Midweek*, July 27, 1988, pp. 30–31. [From a letter dated January 17, 1955.]

Poems

"Biography": *Poetry* 50 (September 1937): 327.

"The Manifesto of Human Events," "Surely the Living Departed," and "The Shadow of a Tear": in *Chorus for America: Six Filipino Poets*, ed. Carlos Bulosan (Los Angeles: Wagon and Star, 1942), pp. 29–32. Bulosan used the pen name "Cecilio Baroga."

"Blood Music, 1939": *Commonwealth Times* 1: 5 (May 1939).
"Death and Transfiguration": in *Chorus*, p. 39.
"Waking in the 20th Century" (c. 1950): in *Bulosan*, p. 119.
"Letter in Exile": *Poetry* 60 (April 1942): p. 16.
"Portrait with Cities Falling" (c. 1944): in DF.
"For a Child Dying in a Tenement" (c. 1940): in *AAJ*, p. 104.
"The Foreigners": *The Lyric* 15 (Spring 1935): p. 159.
"Needing No Time": *Poetry* 50 (September 1937): p. 328.
"Hymn to a Man Who Failed": in AAJ, p. 105.
"Factory Town" (c. 1935): in *AAJ*, p. 106.
"Meeting with a Discoverer" (c. 1951): In Susan Evangelista, *Carlos Bulosan and His Poetry* (Quezon City: Ateneo de Manila University Press, 1985), p. 152–53.
"Biography between Wars" (c. 1942): in *AAJ*, p. 111.
"If You Want to Know What We Are," in *Literature under the Commonwealth*, ed. Manuel Arguilla et al. (Manila: Philippine Writers League, 1940), pp. 48–50.
"To My Countrymen" (c. 1953): in *AAJ*, p. 112.

Correspondence

"Letters, 1937–55": In *Sound of Falling Light: Letters in Exile*, ed. Dolores Feria (Quezon City: University of the Philippines Press, 1960).
"Letters to an American Woman": in *Carlos Bulosan, Selected Works and Letters*, ed. E. San Juan, Jr., and Ninotchka Rosca (Honolulu: Friends of the Filipino People, 1982): 55–83.
"Letter to a Filipino Woman": *The New Republic* (November 8, 1943): 645–46.

"Autobiographical Sketch": in *Twentieth Century Authors*, ed. Stanley Kunitz (New York: H. H. Wilson Co., 1955): 144–45.

Acknowledgments

I would like to thank Aurelio Bulosan and the University of Washington Libraries for permission to publish this selection of writings by Carlos Bulosan. The late Dolores Feria also granted me the right to use Bulosan's letters. Professor Sucheng Chan deserves credit for accepting this volume, and Bulosan's novel *The Cry and the Dedication*, as part of the series she edits for Temple University Press. I also want to express my gratitude to my colleagues at Bowling Green State University—Delia Aguilar, Karen Gould, Ellen Berry, and Robert Perry—for their valuable encouragement and support. The following colleagues and friends also contributed their share in realizing this project: Alan Wald, James Bennett, Robert Dombroski, Roger Bresnahan, Evelyn Hu-Dehart, Sam Novmoff, Donald Pease, and Arif Dirlik. Readers of Bulosan and students of Asian American culture owe much to the mediation of Janet Francendese, Executive Editor, and the staff of Temple University Press, in the production of this volume. Last but not least, I am grateful to Karin Aguilar-San Juan and Eric San Juan for their solidarity and inspiration.

E. SAN JUAN, Jr.

On Becoming Filipino

Selected Writings of Carlos Bulosan

Introduction

According to the 1990 U.S. Census, the Filipino community is now the second largest Asian American population in the United States, with the greatest number living in the state of California. It is estimated that by the year 2000 there will be over two million Filipinos in this country (Patel). But in the study of contemporary U.S. culture and society and in the multiethnic literary canon, Filipinos simply do not exist—or else they are tokenized and subsumed within the larger, official category of "Asian American." Given the genuine historical, political, and cultural differences between people of Filipino ancestry and other Asian ethnic groups, together with the current interrogation of the hegemonic claims of a unitary "American common culture," I propose that Filipinos and their practice of cultural production should now be appraised as a force in its own right, in its difference and integrity, and in its complex dialectical relationship with the distinctive histories of other peoples of color in the United States, with the dominant consensus, and with the power alignment within the present world system.

One approach to this task of retrieving the Filipino presence in the United States and of locating the space for a process or project called "becoming Filipino" may be to examine the life and writings of Carlos Bulosan. Long forgotten since his brief success in the 1940s, Bulosan was rediscovered in the 1960s by a generation of Filipino American youth radicalized by the antiwar and civil rights struggles. This self-awakening of Filipinos born in the United States arose in conjunction with the worldwide resurgence of "Third World" national liberation movements, particularly in the Philippines. Coinciding with this was the climax in 1965 of the Filipino farm workers' movement led by Larry Itliong and Philip Vera Cruz, and the founding of the United Farm Workers of America (Scharlin and Villaneuva). Initially sparked by an identity crisis, the Filipino youth movement inaugurated the birth of political self-reflection—the "becoming" of a subject claiming to be

1

"Filipino." The reissuance of Bulosan's *America Is in the Heart* (hereafter *America*) in 1973 catalyzed this process of recuperating the past, interrogating the present, and revisioning the future. I shall address the contours of this process in the next sections. With the downfall of the Marcos dictatorship in the Philippines in 1986 and the ascendancy of a neoconservative trend in the United States, however, the energies mobilized by this process have been rechanneled once more into either hedonist or neo–Social Darwinist preoccupations, leaving a sizable number of young Filipinos in the United States growing up into the twenty-first century with no alternative but hedonistic life styles, crass consumerism, and a generally unreflective conformity to the official dispensation.

This impasse in the evolution of the Filipino community in the United States is then the conjunctural pretext for this volume. What does Bulosan, with his sensibility shaped by the Depression of the 1930s and the circumstances of the 1940s and 1950s, have to offer in articulating that still intractable and anarchic desire called "becoming Filipino"? Given the disparity between his peasant/working class background and the petit bourgeois cosmopolitan milieu of recent Filipino immigrants, what in Bulosan's writings can help us understand the unresolved predicament—the powerlessness and invisibility—of being labeled a "Filipino" in post–Cold War America? My intervention here as editor aims less at providing answers to these questions than at establishing a forum for exploring the pertinacity and resonance of such issues, which, in their initial formulations, I wrestled with while writing the first scholarly treatise on Bulosan in 1972 and while editing several collections of his works in the last two decades. The forthcoming publication of Bulosan's novel *The Cry and the Dedication* (hereafter *The Cry*) also seeks to open the space for a dialogue between the first group of Filipinos to immigrate to the United States and those migrant professionals who have arrived since 1965, an exchange made more necessary and urgent today by the resurgence of unprecedented racism in the United States and the intensification of civil war in the Philippines. Whatever our personal biases and situational contingencies, Bulosan will not ignore us, even if we remain indifferent or pretend to be unconcerned.

I

Our destiny
To find our path once again to the heart of the earth. . . .
For it is the power to see beyond ourselves,
And to give ourselves. . . .
    —Carlos Bulosan, "Five Poems for Josephine"

When Carlos Bulosan was born on November 2, 1911, in Mangusmana, Binalonan, Pangasinan, the Philippines was already a full-fledged U.S. colony after Spain's defeat in the Spanish American War of 1898. After the disastrous Filipino American War (1898–1902) that killed an estimated one million Filipinos and several thousand Americans, the United States proceeded to transform this Southeast Asian archipelago into a classic colonial dependency, a source of raw materials and cheap labor power (Constantino). After almost a half-century of nationalist resistance, both peaceful and violent, and three years of savage rule by the Japanese military, the Philippines gained its political independence in 1946.

Unlike China or Japan, the homeland of the Filipino people was an emergent sovereign territory when it was forcibly invaded and annexed by the United States. With the destruction of the first Philippine Republic by 1901, Filipinos were subjugated as "natives," "a semi-barbaric population," in the words of U.S. labor leader Samuel Gompers, destined to be soon "civilized." While such white supremacist ideology informed the U.S. policy of "benevolent assimilation" in the Philippines, the logic of U.S. liberal capitalism dictated a recognition of the long-enduring tradition of indigenous resistance to colonialism, and hence Filipinos continued to be classified as aliens for purposes of U.S. immigration. In 1903 William Howard Taft, the islands' first civil administrator, proclaimed the cooptative slogan "Filipinos for the Philippines," thereby inaugurating the advent of the neocolonial order under which, up to now, thousands of Filipinos continue to migrate to the United States every year.

Except for a few hundred *pensionados,* or students sent by the colonial government to be trained for bureaucratic positions, the first sizable group of Filipinos arrived in U.S. territory in 1907, when 150 workers were recruited by the Hawaii Sugar Planters Association (Chan). From then until 1946, at least 125,000 Filipino workers sold their labor power as commodity to the Hawaiian plantation owners and alienated their bodies to the Alaskan canneries and to West Coast agribusiness. From 1900 to 1946, the Filipinos in the United States were thus neither immigrants in the conventional sense nor settlers; rather they were, in today's parlance, "economic refugees." They were colonized "subalterns" (in Antonio Gramsci's sense of ideologically subjugated groups) whose bodies were transported from the hinterland to the metropolis, whose physiognomies were studied and customs were classified by the appropriate ideological mechanisms (including schoolteachers and Protestant missionaries) in order to legitimize the supremacy of U.S. knowledge/power and its disciplinary regime over an entire nation. Thus, unlike the Chinese and other Asian groups whose first experience of victimization in the United States was mediated by their encounter with immigration authorities, the Filipinos may be considered exceptional among Asian immigrants precisely because of their origin as the objects of U.S. colonial subjugation at once coercive and consensual. In general, the Filipino was the product of what Louis Althusser calls the machinery of "interpellation" in which individuals, addressed by the ideological apparatuses of race, class, and gender, become the subjects/bearers of specific functions within the framework of overdetermined, uneven, and combined modes of production and reproduction geared for worldwide capital accumulation.

Driven by poverty and feudal oppression at home, Filipinos under U.S. imperial tutelage began their travels to the United States to pursue the "dream of success" via thrift, hard work, and unrelenting self-sacrifices (Buaken; Pido). By 1930 there were 108,260 Filipinos all over the country—mostly farm workers on the West Coast—with indeterminate status: neither protected wards nor citizens, they were subjected to various forms of racist discrimination and exclusion, circumscribed by (among others) laws of antimiscegenation and prohibited from employment in government and from ownership of land (McWilliams). Between 1898, with the U.S. annexation of the islands, and 1946, with the establishment of an independent Philippines, Filipinos in the United

States (called "Pinoys") inhabited a limbo of indeterminacy: neither citizens nor complete foreigners, they were "nationals" or colonial wards without a sovereign country. Neither citizens nor strictly aliens, Filipino "nationals" (mostly males) suffered class, national, and racial oppression directed by agribusiness functionaries and administered by technocratic state bureaucracies—the legislature, the courts, and the police. Categorized in this irreconcilable alterity, Filipinos endured as victims of exploitation perpetrated by such forces as labor contractors, farmers, gamblers, and racist vigilantes, state laws (Melendy; Takaki). Deterritorialized in this way, members of this "internal colony" fought to survive and affirm their human rights and dignity. In doing so they forged a rich and complex culture of resistance linking their homeland (site of dispossession) with the metropolitan power (site of commodification). For example, in an action paralleling the endemic revolts of peasants in the colonized islands, in 1919 Filipino workers organized one of the first unions in Hawaii, the Filipino Federation of Labor, which spearheaded multiracial industrywide strikes in 1920 and 1924 (Chan). In 1934, the Filipino Workers Association was established in California, with some two thousand active members; it organized the strikes of 1934 in Salinas, El Centro, Vacaville, and the San Joaquin Valley (referred to in *America*). This reservoir of experience eventually enabled the Filipino Agricultural Workers Organizing Committee to lead the historic grape strike of 1965, the matrix of which became the United Farm Workers of America (Catholic Institute for International Relations).

Equipped only with textbook stereotypes of American society and its affluence, Bulosan landed in Seattle, Washington, in 1930, during the worst economic crisis of the twentieth century: the Great Depression. Laboring in restaurants and farms in those years of poverty, homelessness, and racial antagonisms, he was exposed to the suffering of migrant workers scattered from California to Alaska, and, in the process, learned their survival craft. The Depression inflicted on Filipinos (100,000 in Hawaii, 30,000 in California) severe unemployment, intense labor exploitation, and rampant vigilante violence. In 1928 and 1930, Filipinos were attacked by racist mobs in such places as Yakima Valley, Washington, and Watsonville, California (Bogardus). Filipinos were also threatened with deportation. On top of this, in 1935 immigration from the Philippine Commonwealth was limited to fifty people.

Bulosan's apprenticeship as an organic intellectual of the masses (in Gramsci's sense of leaders who conceptualized their coherent identity) started with the trials of his family to overcome feudal tyranny in a colonized social formation. While Bulosan followed his two brothers, Aurelio and Dionisio, to California in order to escape the hopeless destitution of his village, where unequal property relations were sanctioned by the U.S. colonial power, his life in the West Coast exposed him to the hazards of itinerant work (Kunitz). In the early 1930s, he became involved in union organizing through his friendship with Chris Mensalvas of the United Cannery, Agricultural, Packing, and Allied Workers of America (UCAPAWA); he also participated in the activities of the CIO (Congress of Industrial Organization). He served as editor of *The New Tide* in 1934; this bimonthly workers' magazine brought Bulosan into contact with progressive writers such as Richard Wright, William Saroyan, William Carlos Williams, and Louis Adamic. He also wrote for the *Philippine Commonwealth Times* and two other newspapers in the Stockton and Salinas areas.

When Bulosan was confined in the Los Angeles General Hospital for tuberculosis and kidney problems, it was Sanora Babb and her sister Dorothy who, according to his poignant testimony in *America,* helped him discover through books a new "world of intellectual possibilities—and a grand dream of bettering society for the working man." From 1936 to 1938, the convalescent Bulosan read voraciously the works of Pablo Neruda, Theodore Dreiser, James Farrell, Nazım Hikmet, John Steinbeck, Maxim Gorky, Karl Marx, Walt Whitman, Agnes Smedley, Lillian Hellman, Nicolas Guillen, Edgar Snow, Mahatma Gandhi, George Bernard Shaw, and José Rizal, among others, as well as periodicals like *New Masses, The New Republic,* and *Nation* (Feria). His further adventures in the Los Angeles Public Library completed his rudimentary high school education and endowed him with a working knowledge of human behavior and a grasp of world history. But it was his partisan experience as a journalist and union activist that actually laid the groundwork for Bulosan to become a committed "tribune" (in Lenin's sense of collective spokesperson) of the Filipino people.

The responsibility of the tribune involved the twin tasks of critique and prophecy. Even while in the hospital, Bulosan began composing his vignettes indicting patriarchal despotism (both religious and domestic) and the tyranny of the feudal/comprador elite. He depicted the life-worlds of plebeian rebels and outcasts, outlawed subalterns who bore the stigmata of inhabitants from a dependent economy. These comic-satiric fables would later be collected in the best-selling *The Laughter of My Father* (hereafter *Laughter*) published in 1944. Contrary to the philistine dismissal of this book as commercialized folk humor and mere local "exotic" color, Bulosan himself emphasized its allegorical thrust (its aesthetic decorum is elaborated in his article "I Am Not a Laughing Man"): "My politico-economic ideas were embodied in all my writings. *Laughter* is *not* humor; it is satire; it is indictment against an economic system that stifled the growth of the primitive . . . making him decadent overnight without passing through the various stages of growth and decay" ("Sound of Falling Light" 273 [Other more trenchant stories in which Bulosan attacks the predatory excesses of the oligarchy and the horrors of profit accumulation in the first three decades of U.S. rule of the Philippines are now available in *The Philippines Is in the Heart*.]) By mobilizing folk/plebeian memory and the carnivalesque resources of his heritage, Bulosan devised a strategy of cultural resistance that would subvert the Eurocentric representation of Filipino "Otherness," an alterity captured in his perception that (as he phrased it in a letter) it was "a crime to be a Filipino in America."

Bulosan's art was thus born in the gap between colonial bondage and capitalist "freedom." His obsessive theme revolves around the Filipino people's attempt to deconstruct their anonymity/subordination and thus gain autonomy, the power of self-determination. To help perform a cognitive-ethical mapping of the future as a space of national emancipation and attainment of full "species being" (Marx's term), in his works Bulosan seeks to harness ideas, dreams, memories, and images flashing in moments of danger to reconstitute the ideals of the aborted 1896 revolution and numerous insurrections thereafter. In this process he memorializes the figure of the resolute, strong, persevering mother (see, for instance, "Passage into Life" or the first part of *America*) associated with planting/harvest rituals. He celebrates the beauty and fertility of the homeland that, amid his panicked flight from lynchers and police, become symbolic of an immanent harmony, relics of a fugitive but incarnate happiness. This cathexis of the soil/mother imagery serves as a counterpoint to the linear rhythm of historical development and generates the tension of semantic horizons in Bulosan's narratives. When the mystique of kinship dissolves and the promise of security and heirs vanishes, the Filipino worker discovers multiple affinities with his compatriots and recuperates the submerged impulse of racial/national solidarity in the wasteland of capitalism: gambling houses, labor barracks, union halls, and brothels. While exploding the illusion of mobility, the mythical "dream of success," these tabooed, peripheral sites become the matrix of Bulosan's historical imagination, which extrapolates from the past, from loss, and from expenditure, the emerging free play of mutual recognitions. Eventually the Filipino finds allies and collaborators among white workers, middle-class women in particular, and other nationalities and races participating in picket lines, strikes, and other militant struggles for justice and equality.

Before that crisis of global capitalism known as the Great Depression ended, Bulosan had already plotted out his long-range program of anatomizing the political economy of the colonized psyche. His mandate was to "interpret the soul of the Filipinos. . . . What really compelled me to write was to try to understand this country [the United States], to find a place in it not only for myself but my people" (*Selected Works* 81). "Self" here does not mean the paranoid denizen of Lacan's Imaginary register (before assumption of a social identity in the symbolic realm), that phase of psychic development characterized by identifying the self with illusory models. Instead it not only alludes to the Filipino ethnic particularity but also envisages a nascent collective agency of all subordinated people inventing new forms of subjectivity. Such a place in the U.S. cultural canon and public consciousness has yet to be claimed and staked out by people of color following in Bulosan's wake.

II

And all will move forward
On the undiscriminate course of history that never
Stops to rectify our tragic misgivings and shame.

—Carlos Bulosan, "Letter in Exile"

We are not pure in blood but one in living deed.

—Carlos Bulosan,
"Meeting with a Discoverer"

On the eve of Pearl Harbor, Bulosan summed up his years of experience as a union propagandist/agitator and nomadic exile: "Yes, I feel like a criminal running away from a crime I did not commit. And the crime is that I am a Filipino in America. . . . It was now the year [1941] of the great hatred; the lives of Filipinos were cheaper than those of dogs" ("Sound of Falling Light" 199). This moment signals the birth of the writer's dialectical sensibility. We observe Bulosan's totalizing urge to inventory what had been achieved by the popular resistance in the Philippines to the oppression of the first three decades of U.S. colonial rule. When "life was swift and terrible," Bulosan had to repudiate liberal individualism and the hubris of the intellect. He was compelled to realize that without the organized resistance of the working masses and the discipline of cooperative labor, the individual is condemned to recapitulate the ignominy of the past: the painful vicissitudes of colonial servility and self-contempt as well as the atrocities of the 1930s, when Filipinos in the United States were stigmatized, quarantined, and lynched.

The exemplary text of such a counterhegemonic strategy is *America*, Bulosan's novelistic synthesis of Filipino lives written in the middle of World War II. Because of its centrality in the Bulosan canon, its popularity, and its problematic challenge to the critical consensus, I will sketch here an approach to this text that may serve also as a framework for appreciating the selections of his stories, poems, essays, and letters in this book.

Originally acclaimed as one more testimony of immigrant success when it appeared in 1946, *America* in fact presents a massive documentation of the varieties of racist discrimination, ostracism, exploitation, and wholesale dehumanization suffered by Filipinos in the West Coast and Alaska in the decade beginning with the Depression up to the outbreak of World War II. Scenes of abuse, insult, neglect, brutalization, and outright murder of these colonial "wards"—aborigines of the United States's only directly governed colony in Asia—along with examples of their craft of survival and resistance are rendered with naturalistic candor. The bulk of the narrative charts the passage of Allos, the youthful protagonist (Bulosan's persona), who doubles as narrator/ participant and witness, in a land of privation, terror, and violence. It begins with his victimization by corrupt labor contractors on his arrival in Seattle, his anguished flight from a lynching mob, and his first beating by two policemen in Klamath Falls—vicissitudes punctuated in the middle of the book by his testicles being crushed by white vigilantes (208). A hundred pages after this episode replete with more degrading ordeals, Allos concludes by reaffirming his faith in America. How do we reconcile this stark discrepancy between reality and thought, between fact and ideal? Is this simply an ironical tactic to syncopate naïve narrator with subversive author (Alquizola)? Are we in the presence of what's undecidable, a simultaneous gesture of deferring and differing meant to trigger deconstructive *jouissance*, an intermittent self-forgetfulness induced by the pleasure of reading?

One way to resolve this tension is to reject the conventional thesis that *America* belongs to "that inclusive and characteristic Asian American genre of autobiography or personal history" (Kim 47) intended to promote a vacuous agenda of pluralism in the marketplace. In my view, Bulosan invents here a new genre, the antithesis to the quest for assimilation. The address to the "American earth" at the end is cast in the subjunctive mode, sutured in an unfolding process whose future is overshadowed by Pearl Harbor and the defeats in Batan and Corregidor. The last three chapters insistently rehearse the bitterness, frustration, loneliness, confusion, "deep emptiness," and havoc in the lives of Filipinos in America. Critics have alleged that because of the pressures of the Cold War and the publisher's marketing ploy, Bulosan was forced to disseminate in the text praises of American democracy sharply at odds with his message of almost total victimization. I suspect there is some truth to this charge, but what demands clarification is how we are able to perceive the discrepancy and assay the text's "cunning" in using alternating perspectives to convey something more complex. However, to construe Bulosan's chronicle of the Filipino endeavor to salvage dignity from damaged lives as an advertisement of majoritarian "nationalism" (Fuchs) or as an exhibitionist pluralism (Lim) is quite unwarranted. This publicity, however well-intentioned, works to erase all evidence of the book's profoundly radical, anti-Establishment motivation.

Perhaps the easiest way to elucidate this crux is to highlight the trope of personification, the wish-fulfilling Imaginary of this artifact. Who is "America"? Bulosan replies in his text: Eileen Odell, one of his companions and mentors, "was undeniably the *America* I had wanted to find in those frantic days of fear and flight, in those acute hours of hunger and loneliness. This America was human, good, and real" (235 [on Bulosan's relations with American women, see Evangelista]). If "Eileen" and her surrogates function as a synecdoche for all those who demonstrated comradeship to a stranger like Bulosan, then the term should not to be conflated with the abstract referent "U.S.A." as a whole. Overall, the caring maternal figure with her multiple personifications (the peasant mother, Marian, the Odell sisters, Mary, and others who serve as icons of mutual recognition) is the singular desire thematized as "America."

Viewed from another angle, the idiomatic tenor of the title may be read as a metaphor of an inward process of self-becoming and more precisely of parthenogenesis: it is in Bulosan's "heart"/sensibility that "America" (the text) germinates. By metonymic semiosis, the trope of containment gestures toward deliverance: discovering he could write after striking back at the white world and feeling free, Bulosan translates his life into the text of *America*. Of crucial importance is his equation of "heart" with "one island" (323), the Philippines. Literally and figuratively, then, the "heart" becomes a polysemous vehicle that signifies either inclusion or exclusion—a fantasy/romance metaphor (what Mikhail Bakhtin calls a "chronotope," or a space-time configuration) integral to the task of adumbrating a community within the treacherous, alienating, heartless metropolis.

This utopian theme of imagining a home, an extraterritorial enclave, within the fold of a disintegrated polity explains the didactic portions of *America*. The climax of Bulosan's project of educating his fellow Filipinos about the unifying trajectory of their fragmented lives allows him to displace their hopes into the vocabulary of America as "our unfinished dream" (312). Purged of his narcissistic malaise, he writes, "I was rediscovering myself in their lives." This counters the Robinson Crusoe motif of individualism and replaces it with the Moses/mother motif of collective concern. The narrator's private self dissolves into the body of an enlarged "family" (recall that he originally traveled to America to find his brothers and thus reconstitute his broken family) whose members are affiliated by purpose or principle, anticipating what Bulosan calls "the revolution . . . the one and only common thread that bound us together, white and black and brown, in America" (313). The ideal of fraternity among races (nurtured by the fight against a common global enemy, fascism) grounds the virtues of patience and hope underlying his "prophecy of a new society." This ideal can also be conceived as a "structure of feeling" that motivates the narrator's obsession with the Spanish Civil War, the key historical conflict polarizing events and characters, and adding a touchstone of authentic solidarity. Framed by Bulosan's cathartic discovery of his ability to write and his acquisition of a socialist vision of "the war between labor and capital" ("Labor and Capital" 1), the apostrophe to the multiracial masses as "America" gravitates around a cardinal principle: the unity of all the oppressed across class, gender, and racial lines precedes the restructuring of state power. This appeal to "America," a word whose meaning is subject to constant renegotiation, is better grasped as part of Bulosan's strategy to rearticulate the liberal discourse of civil rights toward a socialist direction. This of course incurs risks and liabilities, hence the quoting of "America" as a double bind.

What thus makes *America* the first example of a new genre—a popular-front allegory that articulates class, race, nation (ethnicity), and gender in a protean configuration—is its narrative schema. The stages of Bulosan's awakening follow a path away from a focus on "workerist" unionizing to a concern with broader social issues in a force-field of diverse collectivities. This is the thrust of the plot of "becoming

Filipino," the odyssey of a young native who matures into an artist; the vocation of writer is realized through imperial, racist violence, which is paradoxically also the condition of possibility for his art. By the time Bulosan joins the socialist-oriented union movement and helps edit *The New Tide*, he has already acquired a consciousness able to comprehend the world through a historical-materialist optic, a philosophy of revolutionary praxis transcending family, ethnic chauvinism, and nation. Against the tribalism of government representatives, Bulosan counterposes a socialist outlook informed by the ecology of heterogeneous civilizations. He is cured of the symptoms of the Hegelian "Unhappy Consciousness" exemplified in *America*.

What any reader will have noticed by the middle of the book is how its realistic style and its affinities with picaresque naturalism (recurrent scenes of petty crimes, squalid surroundings, raw violence, and rough language) are frequently disrupted by lyricized memories of the homeland. At this point, the generic norms of the memoir and confession, with their penchant for chronological verisimilitude and linear plotting, have already been eroded by a subterranean comic rhythm of repetition: characters appear and disappear with uncanny resilience and gusto, incidents multiply and replicate, while the narrator's comments and the dialogue he records are disaggregated, shuffled, and redistributed in a circulation of energies that thwart the drive for organic unity. The crisis of hegemonic representation ripens at this juncture.

In Part III of *America*, a decisive break occurs that cancels out the model of the successful immigrant and its corollary "melting pot" archetype: Bulosan's "conspiracy," or dream of making "a better America," a forgetting of the Filipino unconscious, is suspended by the breakdown of the body—a product of years of hunger, isolation, and terror. His hospitalization concretizes U.S. hospitality. History, the incommensurable waste of injustice, materializes in the return of the "child" as invalid; the time of drifting and wandering metamorphoses into the stasis of physical breakdown. In retrospect, Bulosan's illness is not a slight-of-hand interruption but a functional device. It halts the spatial discontinuity, the alleged "Necessitous mobility" (Wong 133), of the narrative line. His illness also ushers him to a recognition (the numerous recognition scenes in the book comprise the comic refrain that brackets individualistic fatality and environmental determinism) of his new vocation: not so much the ignored author of *Laughter* (an index of Bulosan's acknowledgment of the folk sources of his art) as the ventriloquist of collective memory and guardian of the covenant with the "associated producers" of the islands. We encounter finally the limit of liberal idealism.

But what constitutes the originality of the text—yet something no one has so far noticed—is its rendering of what Julia Kristeva calls "women's time," virtually the subtext of Filipino self-constitution. Comedy and the flows/flights of the unconscious interact with the realist code in defining this new genre. The fundamental mythos of comedy, the alternation of death and rebirth in "monumental" time, organizes the allegory of a transported native who "died many deaths" in his itinerary of exile and fantasized return. The suicide of the writer Estevan precipitates in the protagonist a mutation, a turnaround: "I began to rediscover my native land, and the cultural roots there that had nourished me, and I felt a great urge to identify myself with the social awakening of my people" (139). These deaths impregnate the psyche, inducing the self-production of the text noted earlier, recovering the ruins of archaic plenitude in the language of dreams.

Earlier I called attention to how Bulosan deploys the theme of popular-front democracy versus fascism (Japanese aggression in the Philippines eclipses the earlier invasion by the United States) at the outbreak of World War II to negotiate the tension between náive idealism and realist mimesis. He also utilizes this conflict to induce amnesia of the U.S. imperial conquest of the Philippines. This alliance with bourgeois democracy is achieved at the expense of almost forgetting the primal event of colonial conquest and deracination, hence the compulsive repetitions of scenes/events in the narrative. Bulosan testified that as rootless exiles "socially strangled in America," Filipinos find it easier "to integrate ourselves in a universal ideal." But a dialectic of compensatory fulfillment insinuates itself when the fact of colonial domination registered in feudal and comprador rule becomes the repressed, hermeneutic *sine qua non* of the text.

Indeed, what most readers of *America* have ignored by virtue of dogmatism or inertia is the whole of Part I, in particular the resourcefulness, perseverance, and courage of the peasantry, which could not be fitted into an implicit Asian American canonical paradigm. U.S. imperial subjugation of the Philippines is what even scrupulous scholars have forgotten, an omission that is bound to haunt them. What the rhetoric of the book wants to elide but cannot, the absence or lacuna whose manifold traces everywhere constitute the text, is the U.S. colonial violence—the Philippine American War of 1898–1902 and its legacy as manifested in the patronage system—that subjugated the natives, reinforced the oppressive structure Bulosan called "absentee landlordism," and drove him and tens of thousands of Filipinos to permanent exile. Its other name is "fascism," whose genealogy includes Spanish Falangists and their Filipino sympathizers, American racist vigilantes and police, and Japanese aggressors—the last evoking what the text dares not name: U.S. invasion of the islands at the turn of the century. This is what the text's archaeology of reiterations seeks to capture: the scenario of beginning and apocalypse, of loss and recovery; the time of the islands, of the mother and all the women who have been victimized by phallocentric law and custom. What *America* attempts to transcribe in "women's time," whose exorbitance is measured, calculated, and dispersed into the fault lines of the American landscape where derelict Filipinos—including the conflicted witness named Bulosan—found themselves "castrated" under the regime of violence.

The project of *America*, then, is the reinscription of this inaugural moment of dispossession/symbolic mutilation in the hegemonic culture by a text that violates all generic expectations. It is a discourse that foregrounds the labor of mutual recognition, collective praxis, and maternal sensibility against the Manichean theologizing of the "Other," the logic of capital. This text as cultural practice valorizes the oppositional, the negative, and the utopian denied by a utilitarian, commodity-centered society. What is needed is to clarify the process whereby the unity of opposites (for example, individual rationality versus tradition) shifts into the protagonist's agon, a unique ordeal of unearthing duplicities and ambiguous causalities, and of discriminating what is fraudulent from what is genuine. Finally, the text interrogates all readers with the following ethicopolitical reflection in its penultimate chapter: "Our world was this one, but a new one was being born. We belonged to the old world of confusion; but in this other world—new, bright, promising—we would be unable to meet its demands" (324). Bulosan's species of wayward realism allegorizes this radical transformation from the old to the new, that is, from colonial bondage redeemed via analysis/critique to witness/judge of that history of decolonization, the project called here "becoming Filipino." This task is accomplished by this writerly document and without the luxury of consolation afforded by the blandishment of traditional aesthetic form.

III

Can you read the secrets of history in my face?
—Carlos Bulosan, "The Shadow of the Terror"

We are the living dream of dead men everywhere,
the unquenchable truth that class-memories create . . .

—Carlos Bulosan,
"If You Want to Know What We Are"

Charting in *America* the evolution of his life from childhood to the outbreak of World War II, Bulosan succeeds in establishing connections between the multiracial proletarian movement in the United States and over four hundred years of dissidence, protests, and revolts against colonial impositions in the Philippines. His mosaic of Filipino lives pays homage to the grassroot initiatives found, for example, in the 1931 uprising of peasants in Tayug, Pangasinan, which may be interpreted as an anticipatory emblem for the strikes of multiethnic farm workers in Hawaii and the West Coast. This nexus in turn ruptures U.S. jingoist patronage. *America,* now a classic text of vagrancy and failure, becomes implicitly a critique of the official assimilationist ideology, the paradigm of immigrant success, that apologists of free-enterprise individualism continue to uphold, a teleology that up to now serves to underwrite the distortion and/or exclusion of Bulosan and other Filipino artists from the mainstream cultural archive. Only a change in the global circumstances that produced their works can undo this status quo.

Profound geopolitical changes separate *America* and its popular-front milieu from the post–Cold War situation of the 1990s. Are fascism and racism dead? Or do we see their resurrection in new disguises? In any case, today I would stress Bulosan's serviceableness as witness to and conscience of that transitional passage in Filipino life in the United States. Bulosan returns to what Amilcar Cabral calls "the source" to recover a submerged tradition of indigenous revolutionary culture, the deeply rooted insurgent ethos of workers, peasants, and intellectuals against imperial racism and violence. He recalls the 1931 Tayug peasant uprising against landlords, merchant compradors, and bureaucrats—local agents of the American suzerain—and, before that, the 1896–98 Filipino insurrection against Spain. One leader of the Tayug uprising, Pedro Calosa, was in fact a veteran of the 1924 strike of Filipino workers in the Hawaiian plantations (Sturtevant). It seems a not wholly fortuitous coincidence that Calosa lived in the province of Pangasinan, where Bulosan was born.

Bulosan's adolescent years were deeply influenced by the survival craft of a large, impoverished family barely subsisting on a small plot of land. In his letters collected in "Sound of Falling Light", as well as in *Laughter,* Bulosan describes the earthy, sometimes shrewd, but always carnivalesque spirit of his father trying to outwit landlords, usurers, politicians, and petty bureaucrats in providing for his family. With the father's authority finally dismantled, Bulosan then begins to focus on the quiet, durable resourcefulness of his mother—that "dynamic little peasant woman" who sold salted fish in the public market of Binalonan and nurtured Bulosan's open, stoic, but adventurous spirit. Her image is sublimated in the samaritanic women crisscrossing the fault lines of *America,* miscegenating female companions exuberant with ideas and plans; the force of these heterogeneous characters represent for Bulosan the "other" half of a schizoid America.

In such representative texts as "Be American," "Story of a Letter," and "As Long as the Grass Shall Grow," Bulosan tracks the vicissitudes of migrant alienation and analyzes the predicament of return/self-recovery of the sojourner *manqué.* In the process he also unfolds those scenes of his solidarity with women of various nationalities and other progressive elements occasioned by his search for his brothers, in effect, his search for meaning in his life. Personal anecdotes thus become synecdoches of collective fate.

Since I have already written at length on the import and architectonics of those stories (see, e.g., *Carlos Bulosan* and *Racial Formations*), suffice it to recall the semiotic dynamics of "Be American." Here a Filipino youth's quest for recognition plots his identity on the objective rhythm of seasonal harvests; this precarious modality of existence in turn undermines the concept and fact of the private ownership of land and the private appropriation of the collective fruit of labor (San Juan, *Reading the West*). This alien "national" (Consorcio), however, destabilizes the foundational logos of business society and must be put in his place. Somehow Consorcio becomes a journalist fighting for the rights of everyone, "native or foreign born," and goes to jail for his ideas of freedom and peace—the substitute for the citizenship he had originally wanted. In a concluding note, the narrator (Consorcio's friend) pronounces an elegiac hymn to the land, "a great mother . . . rolling like a beautiful woman with an overflowing abundance of fecundity and murmurous with her eternal mystery." By way of such unexpected metonymic displacements, Bulosan reminds us of the relevance of Gilles Deleuze's insight that "a society or any collective arrangement is defined first by its points or flows of deterritorialization," its lines of flight (233).

To illustrate further the distinctive cultural praxis embodied in Bulosan's fiction, I offer brief comments on two stories included in this volume, "Passage into Life" and "I Would Remember." They display Bulosan's mode of using the technique of montage to deconstruct the raw materials of experience and reshape them into a teaching-learning artifice, or "organon" (to use Bertolt Brecht's term), so as to provoke critical reasoning. This tactic of defamiliarization is performed through the genre of allegory/fantasy, which is designed to undermine the convention of mimetic realism or at least unsettle the axioms of orthodox formalism. One virtue of this mode lies in its capacity to subtly fuse two antithetical tendencies, a distanced "imitation" of action and the narrator's passionate critique, thus permitting the exercise of both judgement and sympathy at the same time. While we grasp difference, we also apprehend the possibilities of synthesis, however heuristic and provisional, which ultimately enable agency and historic intervention.

Just as *America* evinced in its fabric the problems of fragmentation and fetishism in a market-centered polity, "Passage into Life" and "I Would Remember" evoke and in the process deconstruct them. In the first story, key events in Allos's life from the time he was five to fourteen register the ravages of feudal greed, suicide, clan violence, poverty, and gratuitous cruelty. It depicts the child's initiation into the reality of a disenchanted world characterized by prejudice and the cash nexus. How can he survive and continue to trust and hope? Not only the boy's intimacy with nature (section 2) but also his compassion for the weak (sections 5, 6, 12) enables him to confront the catastrophic loss of his father. The narrator's choric voice foreshadows the encounter with the figure of the stranger and the utopian denouement: "Oh, Allos, hide in the thorns and thickets of the world! . . . Oh, Allos! don't be afraid! The good earth will comfort you in her dark womb!" His greatest fear—his mother's death—is displaced by his concern for the plight of his sister and of the old Chinese man beaten to death; his cry to the dead man—"Wake up, old man. I will tell you we are the same!"—signifies a release from archaic dependency on parent and kins. By juxtaposing scenes of violence and despair with images of solidarity or communion with the natural world, this seemingly arbitrary sequence of episodes sets up the stage for Allos's acceptance of the stranger/prophet whose voice echoes the Enlightenment principles of "life, liberty, and the pursuit of happiness": "No one is really an orphan as long as there is another man living. As long as there is one man living and working and thinking on the earth." And so the knowledge of death's nonfinality inspires Allos to transvalue his life with a totalizing choice: "Now Allos knew: there in the known world he must go to seek a new life, seek it among the living until he would have enough time to pause and ponder on the mystery of the dead" with "a song of joy warming his whole being until it became the song of all his living dreams." While the figure of the welcoming stranger and the parable in the mountain might suggest a transcendence remote from worldly engagements, what needs foregrounding is how the episodic pattern itself logically produces the strangeness (degrees of alienation and the unknown) and the dialogic contract (the boy seeking answers) that coalesce into the emancipatory vision of the last section of "Passage into Life."

A variation of this defamiliarizing method is enacted in "I Would

Remember." Here the problem is how to frame and distance what would otherwise be a horrifying, even morbidly disgusting scene of Leroy's mutilation: genitals cut, left eye gouged, tongue "sliced into shreds," and entrails "spread on the cool grass." Leroy's slaughter by vigilantes, his "screaming like a pig about to be butchered," was witnessed by the "I" together with several compatriots. The drift toward sensational naturalism is checked here by the narrator, who identifies Leroy as a "stranger" preaching unity and whose life manifests a charismatic aura that detaches the body from the spirit. Leroy, testifies the narrator, "had a way of explaining the meanings of words in utter simplicity, like 'work' which he translated into 'power,' and 'power' into 'security.' I was drawn to him because I felt that he had lived in many places where the courage of men was tested with the cruelest weapons conceivable." Hence Leroy's dismemberment proves the power of unity: individuals become a community in the act of sharing and struggling together.

Violence thus yields a vision of communicative rationality and a ritual of exchange. Bulosan pursues here the task of linkage, the suturing of that cleavage or split between the uncertainties of life in the United States and the struggle for freedom and dignity in the colonized Philippines. How does history materialize in that fissure between past and present, between the domain of affection and the territory of alienation? What lines of flight can rescue the adolescent soul in its solitary passage? We are engaged at the outset with two traumatic childhood experiences: the mother's dying at the birth of his brother and his father's killing of the carabao. Although the grandmother's love and sensuous nature assuage the boy's grief, the spectacle of the carabao's slaughter triggers panic: "I wanted to strike my father, but instead, fearing and loving him I climbed out of the pit quickly and ran through the blinding rain to our house."

In the United States, the narrator encounters two deaths before Leroy's in which he discovers a complexity that exceeds the metaphysics of naïve humanism: with Marco, it was his sincerity, honesty, and gift of laughter; with Crispin, it was his gentleness coupled with a redemptive promise, an epiphany of home in exile. Regarding Crispin, "There was something luminous about him, like the strange light that flashes in my mind when I sometimes think of the hills of home. He had been educated and he recited poetry with a sad voice that made me cry. He always spoke of goodness and beauty in the world." The personalities of Marco, Crispin, and Leroy and their deaths reproduce that uncanny oscillation of fear and love the narrator felt for his father, who possessed the authority to castrate and kill. We sense in the tone of the discourse not only resignation and intense watchfulness but also the will to affirm something that survives bodily contingency: "When I saw his cruelly tortured body, I thought of my father and the decapitated carabao and the warm blood flowing under our bare feet. And I knew that all my life I would remember Leroy and all the things he taught me about living." What is achieved by this method of analogic rendering in both stories is not just verisimilitude but also a stance or susceptibility that can absorb the negative and at the same time convert it into material for one's growth. Loss and expenditure become occasions for self-renewal. By probing for contradictions and intervening in the politico-ethical dilemmas of all the victims of democracy, Bulosan's art takes up the challenge of fragmentation, anomic dispersal, reification or reduction to exchange-values, and other dehumanizing symptoms of the Filipino "Babylonian captivity" in the United States.

IV

You too were the face of the land, the tongue
Of the people, the voice of time.
> —Carlos Bulosan, "Who Saw the Terror"

They are even afraid of our songs of love, my brother.
> —Carlos Bulosan,
> "Song for Chris Mensalvas' Birthday"

When the Japanese struck Pearl Harbor in 1941 and subsequently occupied the Philippines, Bulosan "rediscovered" his homeland as the fountainhead of his creative originality and strength. It was not just a mere return to a mythical origin, a sublation or inversion of the past. He illuminates this conversion experience in "My Education": "I realized how foolish it was to believe then that I could define roots in terms of places and persons. I knew, then, that I would be as rootless in the Philippines as I was in America, because roots are not physical things, but the quality of faith deeply [ingrained] and clearly understood and integrated in one's life." In short, roots were "not physical but intellectual and spiritual things," a common faith that Bulosan found in the socialist tradition, a vision of empowering "the wretched of the earth" (in Frantz Fanon's phrase) that transcends nation-state boundaries.

While Bulosan reaffirms the dedication of his work to "the cause of my own people," he also asserts that his writing is not self-sufficient and that his sensibility had been nourished by the praxis of class struggles: "I drew inspiration from my active participation in the workers' movement. The most decisive move that the writer could make was to take his stand with the workers" (*Selected Works* 35). These sentiments and thoughts were underscored in his contributions to the *1952 Yearbook* of the International Longshoreman's and Warehouseman's Union (ILWU), in his "Letter to a Filipino Woman" and "The Writer as Worker," and in the two letters to his nephews written in 1948. In the latter Bulosan, expropriating "the Name of the Father," expressed the paramount motivation for his work by resurrecting the primal scene of wholeness before deracination occurred—an imagined exodus from captivity. I would privilege these texts where Bulosan enunciated first principles as guiding coordinates for any just, rigorous, and substantive appreciation of his achievement.

Earlier Bulosan had written verses in sympathy with the Loyalist defenders of the Spanish Republic, then beleaguered by reactionary forces. He personified his internationalist creed in the character of Felix Razon—otherwise known as Felix Rivas in *The Cry*—who connects the peasant uprising in Tayug (described in *America*) with the Loyalist cause in Spain. Bulosan's commitment to a "popular front" against capitalism in its fascist phase (confirmed by the expansionist militarism of Germany, Italy, and Japan) afforded him a philosophical orientation that gave coherence and direction to the nomadic plight he shared with others. An islander stranded on inhospitable shores, Bulosan was desperately searching for the "heart," or destination, of his journey; he found it in the Spanish Civil War, the prelude to World War II. During the war he affirmed his partisanship via orature and polemic, resulting in three books: *Chrous for America* (1942), *Letter from America* (1942), and *The Voice of Bataan* (1943); the latter was broadcast overseas by the U.S. Office of War Information. Invited by the exiled government of the Philippine Commonwealth to work in its Washington office, Bulosan instead opted to remain on the "battlefront" of union organizing. Meanwhile, he contributed to numerous magazines, among them *New Masses, Harper's Bazaar, Town and Country, New Yorker,* and *Arizona Quarterly.* In my opinion, Bulosan's craftsmanship in the prose genres (fiction, the reflective or familiar essay, letters) is far superior to his attempts at versification, despite exceptions like "Biography," "In Time of Drought," and "Meeting with a Discoverer." Susan Evangelista has heroically endeavored to present the best case for Bulosan as a "Third World" poet, with an emphasis on themes of alienation, internal colonialism, and the lived experience of Filipino immigrants in general; her argument is vitiated by her downplaying of Bulosan's radical-democratic, socialist vision.

Contrary to the critical doxa, Bulosan's Whitmanesque style exhibited in such poems as "If You Want to Know What We Are" and "I Want the Wide American Earth" is neither typical nor recurrent. The rhetoric of identification and panoramic catalogue found in those two poems, as well as their Filipinized versions in "Land of the Morning" and "Prologue," springs from the will to valorize the power of multitudes. The poet envisages serial monads in a market society converging into an irresistible force for change: "we are the subterranean subways/of suffering; we are the will of dignities;/we are the living testament of a flowering race" ("If You Want to Know What we Are"). But we apprehend that behind this impulse is the quest for secular transcendence, for pleasure-filled alternatives invested in the hitherto unacknowledged labor of "deathless humanity." Except for the instrumental or programmatic verses like *The Voice of Bataan* and the unfinished drama *José Rizal,* Bulosan's poems configure the Horatian injunction to instruct (*prodesse*) and delight (*delectare*) with what I would call the pathos of the folkloric sublime that defines his unique poetic signature.

A majority of his poems meditate on the difficulty of representing the nuances and indeterminacies of exile. They strive to delineate the anxious maneuverings of the native caught in the ravaged cities of the Depression, alarmed by the barbarism of war; his predicament inheres partly in his failure to contrive an objectifying equivalent to his apprehension of disaster. "Biography Between Wars," for instance, stages the reminiscence of the halcyon past in which the death of a friend's husband in Teruel, Spain, and the carnage of war can only be filtered through a surreal perspective: "Then the planes swarmed like swallows/And ripped the night with lilies of screaming fire." Reification blights urban life in "For a Child Dying in a Tenement" anguished by the "terror of plenty." In "Portrait with Cities Falling," the speaker's spiritual crisis is rendered with phantasmagoric intensity; his portrait of an industrial wasteland, however, can only evoke a prophetic longing: "Will they [the headless man and the starlight woman] come to remake the world?" "Letter in Exile" escapes this difficulty of representation via the detour of self-estrangement: the speaker transports himself back to the peaceful islands threatened by enemy planes and then recounts his identification with Jews, Negroes, and beauty ravished by power, greed, and "the naked blasphemies of money." He counsels his brother: "But all this will come to pass . . . ."

Meanwhile, in "Waking in the Twentieth Century," Bulosan mediates the exile's predicament by summoning the image of his father, patient and hopeful, plowing the soil against the background of worldwide destruction. At the end he confides to his woman friend that "there will be days when we will stand together," mindful of the antimiscegenation law against Filipinos. As he is overwhelmed by chaos everywhere, the language of his poems during this period becomes repetitive, desultory, extremely uneven. His performance as a poet culminates in a bravado gesture: the act of staking "a claim on the world" in "To My Countrymen": "And across the flaming darkness of life,/I flung a sword of defiance to give you freedom." Here the dramatic protocol of communicating a purpose that will bind the interlocutors together acquires a sublime connotation when the concept or idea— obscured by the contradictions between city and countryside, between the rapturous past and the tormented present, hinted in "Biography Between Wars"—proves unrepresentable. Using these few quotes as touchstones, we can speculate that Bulosan intuited the limits of his poetic skill and range (he was heavily influenced by T. S. Eliot, W. H. Auden, Archibald MacLeish, and other modernists), and chose thereafter to concentrate his energies on cultivating the narrative and expository genres.

But there were also limits of another kind to Bulosan's prosaic sublimations. At the peak of McCarthyism in the 1950s, he was a blacklisted writer (perhaps the only Filipino writer on the FBI's hit list), having mixed with the wrong people such as Chris Mensalvas and Ernesto Mangaong, leaders of the ILWU Local 37, and dangerous subversives who were scheduled for deportation. (For his inspirational poem "I Want the Wide American Earth," Bulosan seized the pretext of the campaign to defend these two scapegoats of the "Free World.") Amid this harassment he continued to pursue his project of revealing connections, building linkages, demonstrating reciprocities, and fostering alliances via the editorship of the *1952 Yearbook* of the ILWU Local 37 (Taverna). In the *Yearbook,* he wrote: "I believe that the unconditional unity of all workers is our only weapon against the evil designs of imperialist butchers and other profiteers of death and suffering to plunge humanity into a new world war" ("To Whom It May Concern," 21).

Amid the Cold War hysteria, how would the government deport this alleged "communist" agitator who had been commissioned by President Roosevelt to write an essay celebrating the "Four Freedoms"? Bulosan's praise of populist democracy, "Freedom from Want" (exhibited at the Federal Building in San Francisco in 1943), fulfilled the imperative of oppositional artists to capture strongholds in the terrain of social reproduction (Benjamin). It succeeded in infiltrating a potentially explosive message that escaped the censors: "But we are not really free unless we use what we produce. So long as the fruit of our labor is denied us, so long will want manifest itself in a world of slaves." Bulosan not only extolled labor and the "desires of anonymous men," but also (with an oblique allusion to a more dangerous manifesto) the right of people to "serve themselves and each other according to their needs and abilities."

By this time (circa 1950s), Bulosan, the author of best sellers like *Laughter* (which had been translated into more than a dozen languages) and *America* (which had been reviewed in the leading periodicals), was internationally famous, listed in *Who's Who in America, Current Biography,* and other directories of notable personalities. In *Twentieth-Century Authors,* his own account of his uprooting and vagrancy—from his birth in the village of Mangusmana, Binalonan, Pangasinan, in 1911 to his life in Los Angeles in the forties—was reproduced without editorial qualification. He anchored his wandering with this conviction: "What impelled me to write? The answer is—my grand dream of equality among men and freedom for all." Bulosan's testimony was lucid, controlled, generous. But his claim may sound banal or premature for an aspiring intellectual from the hinterland whose literary fortune, together with that of a generation of "fellow travelers" and progressive artists around the world, would soon be blasted by the fury of the Cold War. Nevertheless, I think we need to contextualize his ambition in historically specific, differential terms.

For example, the distance between two stories, "To a God of Stone" (1939) and "End of the War" (1944), may be taken as a measure of Bulosan's success in dramatizing the complex predicament of Filipinos (and, metonymically, of all people of color) in the internal colonies of the metropolis. In the earlier story, the narrator's obsession with gambling is interrupted periodically by Dan, a failed and lost spirit whose idiosyncrasies and "strange smell of unknown cities" puzzled the narrator. But Bulosan could not decide whether to focus on Dan's alienation or the narrator's; at one point, his persona muses on his confusion: "What have I done? Where am I headed for? What do I know about the world?" Meanwhile Dan kills two musicians—a gesture of absurd revolt, it seems—but the narrator concludes with the thought of Dan personifying the truth that "man will always be at the mercy of his invisible creations." The inadequacy stares us in the face: Bulosan assumes that a simple mechanical reproduction of his thoughts plus a portrayal of one derelict will be enough to epitomize the decay of bourgeois society. In the later story, however, he succeeds in inventing an "objective correlative" to concretize a large constellation of ideas and feelings. Private Pascual Fidel's dream of the surrender of the Japanese in the Philippines becomes transformed as it circulates into a collective one, a prophecy of the country's liberation overcoming the limits of fetishized individualism (typified by Dan and the musicians): "It was a dream that belonged to no one now." Gambling, the historic index of Filipino victimization, is overcome at every instance when the dream becomes the signifier of exchange between public and private spheres. Meanwhile the American "dream of success" is displaced and its fraudulence exposed as the pathos of subaltern innocence is captured in that telltale idiom of simultaneous acquiescence and vexed refusal:

> Ten years I worked peacefully in America, minding my own business, when the *salomabit* come stabbing me at the back. Maybe it is not much I make, but I got the beautiful Ford from Detroit . . . In the bank I got money—maybe not much, but it is my money. When I see the flag, I take the hat off and I say, "Thank you very much!" I like the color of the flag and I work hard. Why the *salomabit* come? If only I was there!

Mess Sergeant Ponso's anger at having been left out, his conflation of dream and reality, his gesture of self-justification, his sense of futility— all these elements of Filipino "becoming" in that transitional conjuncture may be conceived as precisely what Bulosan's vocation sought to engage with humor and humility. He took his bearings with that reflexive critical distance and political sophistication he had gained in almost two decades of loneliness, suffering, and friendships cutting across the barriers of class, gender, nationalities, and race.

Separation and exile always summon their binary opposites: reunion and return. While Bulosan continued his role as tribune of multiethnic workers (including Euro-Americans) in writing for newspapers like *New Masses* and *Commonwealth Times* (founded by Mensalvas and Bulosan in 1936) as well as for various periodicals in the Philippines, his conscientization widened to embrace the world system in crisis with the entrenchment of fascism in Europe and Japan. Several poems, such as "Portrait with Cities Falling," "Who Saw the Terror," and "To Laura in Madrid," recorded his loyalty to the socialists and anarchists defending the Spanish Republic against Franco's forces. It was easy for him to make the connection between the reactionary authoritarianism of the Falangists, who had the support of Filipino landlords/compradors, and the thugs of U.S. agribusiness, who had the assistance of the state's ideological apparatus (legislature, courts, prisons) and the military (Bulosan, "Manuel Quezon"). His acceptance of a simplistic version of the united-front strategy explains in part the somewhat melodramatic and sentimental paean to pre–U.S. Civil War democracy, as well as his deployment of the utopian metaphor of "America" as a classless and racism-free society, which pervade Bulosan's texts of this period. But all the rhetoric of democracy and the "Four Freedoms" was soon quickly overtaken by McCarthyism.

V

Homeward again under foreign stars. . . .
—Carlos Bulosan, "Landscape with Figures"

Where I knelt, where I wept, where I lived
To change the course of history; because I love you.
   —Carlos Bulosan, "To My Countrymen"

When Japan occupied the Philippines in 1942–44, Bulosan's attention shifted to the popular resistance of another invader—this time perceived as an even more brutal repeat of the Spanish and American conquests. When the Huks (short for "People's Anti-Japanese Army," later renamed "People's Liberation Army") who led the Filipino underground resistance were suppressed by the U.S. military and its puppet regimes, a full-scale people's war erupted in the late 1940s and early 1950s. This period of the Cold War, punctuated by the Korean War, became the time for testing the limits of bourgeois democracy worldwide.

Bulosan reinscribed the exile's predicament in the "problematic" (to use Louis Althusser's term) of "national liberation" in his letters and particularly in his novel *The Cry*, composed in the last five years of his life. This remarkable work, unprecedented in portraying the lives of left-wing guerrillas in the Philippines, was directly inspired by his friendship with the imprisoned vernacular poet Amado V. Hernandez, by his own memory of peasant radicalism in Pangasinan, and by his close association with farm workers in the United States, who were veterans of similar struggles. Moreover, I believe that the Hukbalahap rebel Luis Taruc's autobiography, *Born of the People* (1953), exerted an incalculable influence on Bulosan's thinking, based on his writings of this period.

With the direct intervention of the CIA and the Pentagon in the Philippine military, the United States crippled the Hukbalahap insurgency as part of its global strategy to contain the "communist conspiracy" then ascribed to the Soviet Union and China (Bulosan, "Terrorism Rides the Philippines"). Before the Korean War ended, Bulosan was driven to move beyond the parameters of trade-union reformism (rationalized by the U.S. Communist Party's identification of itself with "Americanism"); he was always looking across the Pacific for signs hovering over turbulent tropical shores. After his stint with ILWU Local 37, he realized that U.S. monopoly capital had become the immediate and long-range threat to the aspiration for justice and independence of Third World peoples. Indeed, the logic of the Cold War compelled Bulosan to reassess his "love affair" with the phantasmal notions of equality and fraternity he had celebrated in *America*. When U.S.-sponsored fascism erupted with renewed virulence in the Philippines, he had no choice but to enact a long-deferred "return" to the primal scene of his dispossession. It was now impossible for him to resuscitate the America of the Puritans and pioneers, whose legitimacy had been rendered suspect, if not refuted and refused, by the transcontinental revolt of people of color, including those in the internal colonies, against Western messianic hegemony headed by the United States. With the symbolic capital of American democracy exhausted, what alternative did Bulosan have?

He makes a wish-fulfilling attempt to respond to that question in the story "Homecoming." The majority of Filipino bachelors who came to the United States in the 1920s and 1930s never returned, for the reason that Mariano, the successful sojourner in this narrative, rehearses in his mind. Paralyzed by anger and fear, however, he is unable to confess the truth: "How could he make them [his family] understand that he had failed in America? . . . America had crushed his spirit." We, the readers, understand the plight of the author's surrogate who, after twelve years in the United States, now believes there is no other place for him in the world but home. A pre-Oedipal fantasy materializes: Mariano "knew that the fate of his mother was in his hands," but as though castrated he lacks some organ for unburdening himself of "all the sorrows of his life." The bliss of return, an eternal moment he has been waiting for, overwhelms him: "The mother was in his arms." Yet he regrets having come home because "he could never make them happy again." After discovering that his father is dead, the reality of his own failure assaults him in the shape of the palpable misery at home:

> Now he could understand his mother's deadening solemnity. And Marcela's bitterness. Now it dawned on him that his mother and sisters had suffered the same terrors of poverty, the same humiliations of defeat, that he had suffered in America. He was like a man who had emerged from night into day, and found the light as blinding as darkness . . . . This was the life he had found in America; it was so everywhere in the world. He was confirmed now. He thought when he was in America that it could not be thus in his father's house. But it was there when he returned to find his sisters wrecked by deprivation.

In Chapter 40 of *America*, Bulosan records a dream analogous to this story that can perhaps help decipher its meaning. Assuming the role of a Filipino communist strike leader fleeing from the police, he falls asleep in a bus and dreams of his return to his hometown in the Philippines, where he rejoices at seeing his mother and the whole family eating; awakened by "tears of remembrance," he claims that the "tragedy" of his childhood returned in a dream "because I had forgotten it" (283). Could this story be an act of remembering, a reenactment, so as to forestall what had already happened? Is the artist's imagination assuming the role of the redeemer/messiah of the past?

In any case, in "Homecoming" Mariano performs a symbolic remapping of the world system when he encounters the depredations of the old enemy in the homeland. The climactic event, graced by "the vision of his father" as he departs—which is ambiguous since Mariano has usurped his place, only to mark it as preempted by someone else—epitomizes the lesson of the homecoming: "America" now turns out to be one huge self-deception. But it is a hard lesson that can only be symptomatically glimpsed, one that assumes full-bodied articulation in Bulosan's last ambitious work, *The Cry*. (Originally he planned to write four massive novels covering one hundred years of Philippine history, a tetralogy meant to rival the mammoth dynasty epics of Honoré de Balzac, Dreiser, and Mikhail Sholokhov.)

In *The Cry*, Bulosan tries to diagnose what happened to him in the United States, and thus the causes of Filipino self-deception and misrecognition. In general, the novel assists in the task of unraveling this mystery, the absent source of the shock in "Homecoming," namely, the uneven topography of the imperial system and its hierarchical power relations. Alternatively one can categorize this absent cause as the totality of class/gender relations on a multinational scale that is fully present in all of Bulosan's writings in the form of damages wrought upon colonial subjects. While in *America* he grappled with the antinomy of the real and the ideal, a tension defused only by the advent of war and the united front against world fascism, its protagonist failed to return (if only by anamnesis) to his origin in the indigenous revolutionary tradition of the Filipino masses. In *The Cry* the return is made.

What *The Cry* deploys is the trope or figural schema of homecoming enacted by members of a guerrilla detachment as preparation for a rendezvous with a certain Felix Rivas, the disfigured bearer/herald of "good tidings" from the United States, whom no one except Dante (the author's alter ego) can recognize. The meeting never takes place. But what this fabula conveys over and above the immense tragedy of Filipino lives is the *szhujet*, or plot, of permanent revolution. This is the subtext in which all characters mobilize the communal "spirit of place" (*genius loci*) of their birthplaces in order to reconstitute their identities by way of wrestling with the demons (promises, disavowals, transgressions) of their individual pasts. Bulosan thus subscribes to Marx's axiom that individuality equals the ensemble of social relations at any given time and place. Through the character of Hassim, Bulosan finally repudiates the aristocratic and even obscurantist idealization of homeland, blood, soil, romanticized childhood, rural harmony, and other kindred mystifications; instead he reaffirms the necessity of collectively rein-venting the future. And through the demise of Dante, a variation of Mariano and other bitter "old-timers," Bulosan induces a catharsis of melancholia, narcissism, and diverse sentimental pieties afflicting the text of *America*. The returned exile Dante, however, fails to make the rendezvous with his other half (the disfigured Felix Rivas) when he is killed by his priest-brother, Father Bustamante, who has never left home. By extinguishing through death the schism in Dante's psyche—Bulosan's trope for the reconciliation of the split psyche, for healing the paranoia and ambivalence complicit in the condition of being an exile/refugee—the authorial intelligence of the novel decides to subsume this problem of the bifurcated subject into the larger goal of enunciating an allegory of national liberation, what Cabral calls "a regaining of the historical personality" of a whole people. By tapping the resources of autochthonous humor, indigenous rituals of resistance, and a popular memory charged with socialized passions and *ressentiment,* Bulosan finally settles accounts with the duplicitous tricksters and sirens inhabiting *America.* His project of "becoming Filipino" in the conqueror's terrain, anticipatory and prefigurative, becomes the only way to realize what the mother, natural abundance, and childhood happiness all represent: freedom, dignity, and recognition of personal worth.

A passage from one of Bulosan's letters may serve to cast light on the title of the novel: "I felt that I would be ineffectual if I did not return to my own people. I believed that my work would be more vital and useful if I dedicated it to the cause of my own people" ("Sound of Falling Light" 259). In an earlier essay, he described the Filipino writer's response to the "twists of history," the "labyrinthine circle of revolutionary upsurge and temporary defeat": "Filipino writers went back to their social roots—the peasantry and the proletariat—and began to weave the threads of their folklore with the national tradition. It was only then that cultural activity became a national consciousness." ("The Growth of Philippine Culture" 12–13). About the time when Bulosan had completed his narrative of Hukbalahap guerrillas articulating their nation's agon in their individual fates, he expressed the fundamental drive of his art in an autobiographical sketch published a year before he died:

> The question is—what impelled me to write? The answer is—my grand dream of equality among men and freedom for all. To give a literate voice to the voiceless one hundred thousand Filipinos in the United States, Hawaii, and Alaska. Above all and ultimately, to translate the desires and aspirations of the whole Filipino people in the Philippines and abroad in terms relevant to contemporary history. Yes, I have taken unto myself this sole responsibility (Kunitz 145).

In one letter, he testified that "what really compelled me to write was to try to understand this country [United States], to find a place in it not only for myself but my people." (*Selective Works* 81). Since he had already exorcised the specter of the American "dream of success," Bulosan was ready to assume a public role. For a decolonizing expatriate like Bulosan, whose vocation is complicit with the destiny of his nation, the responsibility of the writer is "to find in our national struggle that which has a future," particularly in a time of heightened class conflict. Writing then acts as the midwife to cultural renaissance as well as to social transvaluation. The old world is dying, a new world is being born from the ruins of the old—such is Bulosan's crucial insight into the dialectics of historical development. Writing is therefore coeval with the rhythm of the national liberation struggle:

> This is the greatest responsibility of literature in our time: to find in our national struggle that which has a future. Literature is a growing and living thing. We must destroy that which is dying, because it does not die by itself. We must interpret the resistance against the enemy by linking it with the stirring political awakening of the people and those liberating progressive forces that call for a complete social consciousness. ("Letter to a Filipino Woman" 645)

One way of approaching Bulosan's educational value for the generation reared in the hybrid/syncretic milieu of late modernity may be suggested by the tone and disposition of the speaking subject in his letters. One can examine the two letters to his nephews Arthur and Fred (see Campomanes and Gernes) and note how Bulosan seeks to negotiate a dialogue or mutual exchange by imagining the questions and responses of his addressee. He assigns a place of responsibility to Arthur when the image of Arthur's father is evoked as a model of goodness, an inspiration that had sustained Bulosan in his years of degradation—"my life of terror, my defiance against a system that treated human beings like rotten animals." Juxtaposed with this is an aphorism that spontaneously unfolds from the signifiers of mortality (his mother and grandmother): "We will all die: it is only in the affection that we give to each other when we are still alive that keeps the world moving." One other piece of advice is triggered by the sacrifice of Aurelio for his brother Carlos: "Never forget your family, your town, your people, your country, wherever you go. Your greatness lies in them." In the letter to Fred, Bulosan conceives of the "island" ego rejoining the archipelago by choice: "That is real genius: it is not selfish; it sacrifices itself for the good of the whole community." The context of this remark deals with the significance of José Rizal, the Filipino national hero, for the realization of "a free and good Philippines."

While Bulosan plays the mentor and surrogate father in both letters through gestures of advising, recalling scenes of his adolescence, and moralizing about his gambling and the confusion of the times, he never exaggerates his own status; a tone of understatement may be detected in the way he diverts attention from himself to Rizal and Gorky. And even when he boasts of hoping to leave millions of words behind, he urges Fred to remember the writer as one "who herded carabaos in Mangusmana a long time ago." Modulating from local details of memory to fabulation, syncopating the fictive with the exhortative and subjunctive, Bulosan performs an act of healing the mutilated psyche by articulating in his letters the liaisons of self and nation, public and private domains, eros and conscience. Such letters, especially those to his American woman friend, not only substantiate the writer's claims but also release—if we can read between the lines and along the margins—those transgressive forces needed to blast what William Blake called the "mind-forged manacles" as well as those venerable institutions and practices that continue to perpetuate the "nightmare of history" for the empire's multitudes.

In his correspondence gathered in *"Sound,"* we confront Bulosan's alterity, the locus of the civic or "social individual," discernible in this passage from a letter of April 1947: "We are the only expatriates who really lived and worked with the people . . . While we are all alive we must try to understand each other, give each other confidence, help, happiness and goodness." The theme of concern for the Other is further elaborated in a letter to his nephew, where he mentions the approaching death of his (nephew's) mother: "It is good to cry. But don't let sorrow kill your life. We will all die: it is only in the affection that we give to each other when we are still alive that keeps the world moving." In another letter, Bulosan counsels that "we all die . . . any time is as good as any other. . . . But try always to seek the goodness in your fellow man. That is the greatest wealth of all: goodness. And beauty, too. The beauty that you find in all good things."

In spite of Bulosan's reiterated faith in life viewed as "a continuum of desire" where the proportion of empathy and rationality, *dulce* and *utile*, are always shifting, the rumor still persists that Bulosan languished in poverty, alcohol, and obscurity. The whole truth is the opposite. Neither nihilism nor a "sense of foreboding and despair" after the atomic bombs annihilated thousands in Hiroshima and Nagasaki, but a trusting, bold, steady warmth suffuses the following excerpt from a letter of December 1947: "Our task is to live and explore the very roots of life, dig deep into the hidden fountainhead of happiness; and when we die, at last, we must die accepting death as a natural phenomenon and believing also that life is something we borrow and must give back richer when the time comes." Life, not death, obsessed him. Amid the massive destruction of the Korean War and brutalizing counterinsurgency in the Philippines, Bulosan pursued the nomadic stance of proposing alternatives—lines of flight, deterritorializing flows—that were not utopian in the pejorative sense but were in fact heuristic and realizable because they inhered in the actual everyday praxis of life endowed with meaning by the participation of creative, self-determined, responsible, equal citizens.

VI

I can't even dream; the whiteness of the land
Skulks in my sleep, stifling my dream. . . .
—Carlos Bulosan, "The Surrounded"

Sleep peacefully, for your labors are done, your pains
Are turned into tales and songs. . . .
—Carlos Bulosan, "Now That You Are Still"

In his fiction, essays, and poetry, Bulosan interrogated the conjuncture of class, gender, race, and ethnicity that underpins the epochal antagonism between capitalism and various emancipatory, popular-democratic experiments around the world. In retrospect the Cold War offered Bulosan an opportunity to transcend the narrow bourgeois-nationalist program (the Filipino community in the United States can be conceived as an "internal colony," even though it lacked a sizable ghetto or barrio) and move toward a socialist transformation of the empire. In the process, the boundary erected by U.S. hegemony between the Southeast Asian writer/exile and his peasant heritage proved artificial when Bulosan encountered racist exclusion and exploitation in the heartland of capital. Not only *America* but also stories like "The Soldier" and "As Long as the Grass Shall Grow" (the title was inspired by Bulosan's enthusiasm for *Black Elk Speaks*) dramatized the truth that Filipinos suffered not only class disadvantage, racism, and gender discrimination (antimiscegenation laws condemned them to bachelorhood and they were constantly preyed upon by gamblers, sex merchants, and white supremacists of all kinds) but also national oppression. In this the Filipinos shared a predicament similar to that of workers of other races and nationalities. In his voluminous letters, in the novel *The Cry*, in essays like "My Education," "The Growth of Philippine Culture," and "Terrorism Rides the Philippines," Bulosan argues that the Filipino nationality could not exercise its right of self-determination so long as the Philippines was a dependent colony of a power that claimed to be "democratic" but in practice fostered racial, national, and class discrimination. Overthrowing this unjust system meant cutting its stranglehold on people of color in the dependencies and other subordinate formations (the case of Puerto Rico readily comes to mind), still the source of superprofits, cheap labor, and natural resources for transnational corporations.

Earlier I discussed how Bulosan's hitherto neglected novel *The Cry* transports his imagination back to the Philippines to explore what possible ties and reciprocal determinations there might be between peasant-worker insurgency and the Filipino diaspora. One story incorporated in the novel, excerpted here with the title "How My Stories Were Written," rehearses the direction of Bulosan's inquiry. The allegorical resonance of Apo Lacay, the folk sage who resembles the prophet of "Passage into Life," points to the genesis of the historical imagination in the encounter of innocence and experience. Apo Lacay's genealogy brings back to life the primal scene of disinheritance together with the revitalizing power of narrative:

Then it seemed to me, watching him [Apo Lacay] lost in thought, he
had become a little boy again living all the tales he had told us about a
vanished race, listening to the gorgeous laughter of men in the midst
of abject poverty and tyranny. For that was the time of his childhood,
in the age of great distress and calamity in the land, when the fury of
an invading race impaled their hearts in the tragic cross of slavery and
ignorance. And that was why they had all become that way, sick in soul
and mind, devoid of humanity, living like beasts in the jungle of their
captivity. But this man who had survived them all, surviving a full
century of change and now living in the first murmurs of a twilight and
the dawn of reason and progress, was the sole surviving witness of the
cruelty and dehumanization of man by another man, but whose tales
were taken for laughter and the foolish words of a lonely old man who
had lived beyond his time.

The wisdom of folly incarnated in Apo Lacay's sensibility is exemplary
in bridging the gap between the 1898 anti-imperialist resistance to "the
fury of an invading race" and the campaign against the anticommunist
destruction of militant unions and people's organizations in the 1950s.
This mode of apprehending ties, liaisons, and affinities amid disrup-
tions and schisms in the movement's ranks became Bulosan's weapon
of endurance and collective self-transmutation. In twenty years, he had
persevered in mapping the itinerary of the native/alien in the territory
of the metropolis, leaving marks of his ordeal in forging a new, complex
identity for his people, whose novelty and efficacy are still not fully
recognized for reasons already discussed.

In 1937 Bulosan thought he was dying in the city hospital in Los
Angeles. Later he would undergo several more operations for leg cancer
and lung lesions until he was left slightly crippled, one kneecap and one
kidney removed, his body frail and vulnerable. But he lived on until
September 11, 1956, when, after a night of drinking with a labor lawyer
who was a close friend, he wandered around the streets of Seattle; at
dawn he was found sprawled on the steps of the City Hall, "comatose
and in an advanced stage of broncho-pneumonia" (Feria, "Bulosan's
Power" 12). He was a victim less of neurosis or despair than of
cumulative suffering from years of privation and persecution.

Bulosan died at the height of the Cold War, poor but not entirely obscure—the conviviality and stamina of his creative spirit can be discerned in his "Editorial" in the *1952 Yearbook* of the ILWU, where he reaffirmed the union's "uncompromising stand to defend human rights and liberties" against the "maniacal machinations" of the anti-communist witch-hunts. His audience did not fade because postwar prosperity dispelled the appeal of the underdog, but rather because public concern shifted to civil rights and Third World national liberation and thus engendered a new audience. When the Philippines was granted independence in 1946, the need to trumpet America's colonial "success" and win allies for the antifascist cause had already become anachronistic. Bulosan's stories, however, were reprinted in the Philippines and his legendary aura circulated in the labor camps, in the subterranean world of the "old timers," and in radical circles everywhere. In 1965 the Filipino workers in the California vineyards, led by Bulosan's contemporaries Larry Itliong and Philip Vera Cruz, launched the historic strike that led to the founding of the United Farm Workers of America. It was the fruit of dangerous groundbreaking actions initiated in the early 1930s by Bulosan and his associates in the Congress of Industrial Organizations (CIO) and its predecessors.

Bulosan never compromised his principles, his basic commitment to the socialist vision of world revolution. In fact he reaffirmed his conviction at every occasion: "Writing was not sufficient . . . . I drew inspiration from my active participation in the workers' movement. The most decisive move that the writer could make was to take his stand with the workers" (*Selected Works* 35). Little could he imagine in those days of fear and betrayal that after his death he would be vindicated and acclaimed as one of the most eloquent tribunes of the multiracial working class, in the United States and elsewhere; a militant chronicler of the multitudes whose struggles for freedom, equality, and justice would distinguish an era of unprecedented upheavals on the whole planet whose import and significance we are just slowly beginning to understand.

Surveying his life and work in this historical context, I consider Bulosan a formidable revolutionary artist whose contribution to shaping a Third World narrative of people's liberation coincides with his project of resolving the predicament of uprooting and exile, that is, of colonial subjugation. Whether overseas or at home, in all their travels the

Filipinos carried on their backs the burden of history's nightmare. Learning from the rigor of the Depression and the terror of Cold War patriotism, Bulosan worked with others to purge the poison of racist free-enterprise ideology from the mentality and *habitus* of his compatriots. Colonial ideology in general functions as a seductive, self-rationalizing fantasy—the hallucinations of normal common sense, as it were—shrouding the truths of exploitation and racist exclusion; this ideology, Bulosan never tired of pointing out, reproduces and legitimizes the contradiction between the labor of the many who produce social wealth and the control and distribution of that wealth by a privileged minority. Colonial servitude masquerading as freedom can only be remedied by grounding one's life in the practice of separation, distancing, and resistance, and by rooting it in the ethos of a collectivity materializing from the convergence of individual acts of revolt.

As tribune and chronicler, Bulosan engaged in a praxis of committed (tendentious and polemical, if you like) writing intended to persuade, arouse, and instigate readers to action. He sought to integrate the popular struggles in the heartland of colonial power with those in the "uncivilized" and "untamed" hinterlands. His writings may be deemed a cogent witness to the protracted endeavor of the Filipino masses to free themselves from colonial barbarism and from the unrelenting domination of transnational business. In *America* and elsewhere, we observed his radicalization, the ripening of his imagination, transpire in the gap between the ideals of democracy he had been taught and the violence of the reality he experienced. Bulosan was a battle-tested combatant in the confrontation between antagonistic classes and interests on several fronts: between the multinational proletariat and the hegemonic power bloc of transnational capital, between Third World subjects and the elite of the industrialized nation-states. To the end of his life, Bulosan conscientiously strove to fuse both the political imperative of art serving the masses through the popularization of egalitarian principles and the artistic demand for wholeness, delightful release, and magical purposiveness—the ends of usefulness and pleasure. The synthesis he achieved was, in retrospect, an uncompromising but compassionate and lucid critique of the ironies, discrepancies, and paradoxes of Filipino existence in the United States.

Despite his revival in the 1960s and 1970s, and his continuing "prestige" in the field of ethnic studies and other multicultural disciplines, Bulosan actually still remains in the limbo of cultural marginality. Why? Unlike the more notorious Filipino expatriate José Garcia Villa (now rarely read) and despite his limited success, Bulosan was never really accepted by the U.S. literati. One can say that it was Harriet Monroe, editor of *Poetry*, who discovered Bulosan for American intellectuals and ascribed an "American" reputation to him. Given his association with left-wing intellectuals and radical dissidents before and after the Cold War, he was immediately suspect, a fringe or provincial author from the boondocks (from the Tagalog term for mountain, *bundok*). The answer to our question hinges on the powerlessness of the Filipino community in the United States, its "silence" and invisibility, historically predicated on the subordinate position of the Philippines and its dependent status in the world system of late capitalism. Within this global framework, Bulosan cannot be categorized simply as another "ethnic" denizen of the currently thriving multicultural mall. The radicalization of his sensibility from the time he landed in Seattle in 1930 to his death in 1956 enabled him to traverse the boundaries set by the sectarianism of ethnic closure, the nostalgic melancholy of a wish to return to a mythical past, and the elitism of avant-garde arbiters of taste.

Almost two million Filipinos today constitute the second largest Asian American population in the United States, yet their creative force for social renewal is still repressed and unacknowledged. Bulosan endeavored to articulate their presence in his account of multiracial conflicts and individual quests for happiness, insisting, however, on the fundamental primacy of labor or cooperative praxis as the guarantee of liberation for all humans across the barriers of class, gender, nationality, and race. Because of his radical popular-democratic orientation, Bulosan may be regarded as one of the first consciously multicultural writers in the United States whose profound and consistent involvement in anti-imperialist resistance defies assimilation into the hegemonic pluralist canon. (I have cited such attempts at cooptation earlier.) It can also be argued with more credence that he is one of the first "postcolonial" writers who accomplished the task of inscribing the power of the negative—the multiaccentual speech of "Third World" subalterns—in the archive of Western knowledge, questioning its legitimacy, expropriating what was useful, and rewriting the uneven, fractured, dispersed history of the world system from the perspective of its victims.

As long as the Philippines remains a virtual neocolony and the Filipinos an oppressed nationality here and around the world (the diaspora now amounts to five million), Bulosan's texts remain necessary for elucidating the predicament of the Filipino community and its varying modalities of self-affirmation within the political economy of a "New World Order." Bulosan will no doubt form part of the multiracial but still homogeneous map of a complex and rapidly changing society within which the new Filipino settlers in the United States—arriving in numbers of over fifty thousand a year—are bound to regroup, conduct reconnaissance, and recalculate their bearings. The Filipino "alien" will surely find a home in Bulosan's territory, a springboard for future explorations. One of these explorations is that of people of color everywhere claiming their right to be recognized as movers and makers of local/universal history. What Mark Twain at the turn of the century saw as the crucible of the American republic, its feat of subjugating the insurgent Filipinos and thus provoking almost a hundred years of fierce resistance (of which Bulosan's *oeuvre* is one prodigious testimony)—this rich, complex dialectic of exchange, of challenge and response whose configuration I have partly traced here, may prove decisive in inventorying the possibilities and fate of the radical democratic transformation of U.S. society in the twenty-first century.

———————————————

This selection of Bulosan's most representative texts is designed to introduce the general reader to the art and world of a hitherto neglected but extremely important player in the shaping of a U.S. multicultural canon. Bulosan is generally considered the most powerful, authentic voice of the Filipino community in the United States who came in the 1920s and stayed—the first generation of adventurous and daring Filipinos who spearheaded union organizing, helped found the United Farm Workers of America, and contributed to the immense wealth of Hawaii, California, Washington, and the country as a whole.

While essentially introductory, this volume, which includes selections not easily available elsewhere, is more substantial and reliable than any existing anthology. Except for Bulosan's widely disseminated ethnobiography of the Filipino community, *America*, and his collection of comic fables, *Laughter* and *The Philippines Is in the Heart*, this collection presents what I think are his most skillfully crafted fiction, substantive essays, representative poems, and letters (excerpts as well as complete versions, many never published before), which are necessary for understanding the evolution of Bulosan's worldview and appreciating the central themes and organizing principles of his art. Also included is an autobiographical sketch and two letters to his nephews not included in Dolores Feria's edition of Bulosan's letters, *Sound of Falling Light*. (For a more detailed listing of Bulosan's published works, I recommend the May 1979 issue of *Amerasia Journal*, which I helped edit.) All in all, these texts coalesce into a world of the imagination unique in its synthesis of modernity and the resistance of its victims, of Western ideology and a peculiar Third World sensibility, of *pax Americana* and the Filipino reconstitution of its limits and possibilities. Bulosan's novel *The Cry and the Dedication*, with my introduction, is being published as a companion volume to this book by Temple University Press.

Works Cited

Alquizola, Marilyn. "Subversion or Affirmation: The Text and Subtext of *America Is in the Heart*." In *Asian Americans: Comparative and Global Perspectives*, edited by Shirley Hune et al., 199–209. Pullman: Washington State University Press, 1991.

Althusser, Louis. *Lenin and Philosophy and Other Essays*. London: New Left Books, 1971.

Benjamin, Walter. "The Author as Producer." In *The Essential Frankfurt School Reader*, edited by Andrew Arato and Eike Gebhardt, 254–69. New York: Continuum, 1988.

Bogardus, Emory. "Anti-Filipino Race Riots." In *Letters in Exile: An Introductory Reader on the History of Pilipinos in America*, edited by Jesse Quinsaat, 51–62. Los Angeles: UCLA Asian American Studies Center, 1976.

Buaken, Manuel. *I Have Lived with the American People*. Caldwell, ID: The Caxton Printer, Ltd., 1946.

Bulosan, Carlos. *America Is in the Heart*. Seattle: University of Washington Press, 1973. First published 1946.

————. *Chorus for America: Six Filipino Poets*. Los Angeles: Wagon and Star, 1942.

————. "Freedom from Want." *Saturday Evening Post* (March 6, 1943), 15.

————. "The Growth of Philippine Culture." *The Teachers Journal* 9 (May–June 1941): 1–18.

————. "I Am Not a Laughing Man." *The Writer* 59 (May 1946): 143–44.

————. "Labor and Capital: The Coming Catastrophe." *Commonwealth Times* (June 15, 1937): 1.

————. *The Laughter of My Father*. New York: Harcourt, Brace & Co., 1944.

————. *Letter from America*. Prairie City, IL: J.A. Decker, 1942.

————. "Letter to a Filipino Woman." *The New Republic* (November 8, 1943): 645–46.

————. "Manuel Quezon—The Good Fight." *Bataan Magazine* (August 1944): 13–15.

————. "Passage into Life." *If You Want to Know What We Are: A Carlos Bulosan Reader*, edited by E. San Juan, Jr. Minneapolis: West End Press, 1983.

————. *The Philippines Is in the Heart*. Quezon City: New Day Press, 1978.

————. *Selected Works and Letters*, edited by E. San Juan, Jr., and Ninotchka Rosca. Honolulu: Friends and the Filipino People, 1982.

————. "Sound of Falling Light: Letters in Exile," edited by Dolores Feria. Published as a separate volume by the University of the Philippines in 1960. *The Diliman Review* 8. 1–3. (January–September 1960): 185–278.

————. "Terrorism Rides the Philippines." In *1952 Yearbook, ILWU Local 37*, edited by Carlos Bulosan, 27. Seattle: ILWU, 1952.

————. "To a God of Stone." *Amerasia Journal* 6:1 (May 1979): 61–68. Originally published in 1939.

————. *The Voice of Bataan*. New York: Coward McCann, 1943.

————. "To Whom It May Concern." In *1952 Yearbook, ILWU Local 37*, edited by Carlos Bulosan, 21. Seattle: ILWU, 1952.

Cabral, Amilcar. *Return to the Source: Selected Speeches*. New York: Monthly Review Press, 1973.

Campomanes, Oscar, and Todd Gernes. "Two Letters from America: Carlos Bulosan and the Act of Writing." *Melus* 15:3 (Fall 1988): 15–46.

Catholic Institute for International Relations. *The Labour Trade*. London: Catholic Institute, 1987.

Chan, Sucheng. *Asian Americans: An Interpretive History*. Boston: Twayne Publishers, 1991.

Constantino, Renato. *The Philippines: A Past Revisited*. Quezon City: Tala Publishing Services, 1975.

Deleuze, Gilles. *The Deleuze Reader*, edited by Constantin Boundas. New York: Columbia University Press, 1993.

Evangelista, Susan. *Carlos Bulosan and His Poetry*. Quezon City: Ateneo University Press, 1985.

Feria, Dolores. "Bulosan's Power, Bulosan's People." *The Manila Times* (April 28, 1991): 12.

———. "Carlos Bulosan: Gentle Genius." *Comment* 1 (1957): 57–64.

Fuchs, Lawrence. *The American Kaleidoscope: Race, Ethnicity, and the Civic Culture*. Hanover, NH: University Press of New England, 1992.

Gramsci, Antonio. *Prison Notebooks: Selections*. New York: International Publishers, 1971.

Kim, Elaine. *Asian American Literature: An Introduction to the Writings and Their Social Context*. Philadelphia: Temple University Press, 1982.

Kristeva, Julia. "Women's Time." In *The Kristeva Reader*, edited by Toril Moi, 187–213. New York: Columbia University Press, 1986.

Kunitz, Stanley, ed. "Carlos Bulosan." In *Twentieth-Century Authors*, 144–45. New York: H. H. Wilson Co., 1955.

Lim, Shirley Geok-lin. "The Ambivalent American: American Literature on the Cusp." In *Reading the Literatures of Asian America*, edited by Shirley Geok-lin Lim and Amy Ling. Philadelphia: Temple University Press, 1992.

McWilliams, Carey. *Brothers Under the Skin*. Boston: Little, Brown and Co., 1964.

Melendy, H. Brett. *Asians in America*. New York: Hippocrene Books, 1977.

Patel, Dinker I. "Asian Americans: A Growing Force." In *Race and Ethnic Relations 92/93*, 2nd ed., edited by John Kromkowski. Guilford, CT: The Duskin Publishing Group, 1992.

Pido, Antonio J. *The Pilipinos in America: Macro/Micro Dimensions of Immigration and Integration*. Staten Island, NY: Center for Migration Studies, 1986.

San Juan, E. *Carlos Bulosan and the Imagination of the Class Struggle*. Quezon City: University of the Philippines Press, 1972.

———. *The Philippine Crisis*. Hadley, MA: Bergin & Garvey, 1986.

———. *Racial Formations/Critical Transformations: Articulations of Power in Ethnic and Racial Studies in the United States*. Atlantic Highlands, NJ: Humanities Press, 1993.

———. *Reading the West/Writing the East*. New York: Peter Lang, 1993.

Scharlin, Craig, and Lilia Villanueva. *Philip Vera Cruz: A Personal History of Filipino Immigrants and the Farmworkers Movement*. Los Angeles: UCLA Labor Center, 1992.

Sturtevant, David. *Popular Uprisings in the Philippines 1840–1940*. Ithaca: Cornell University Press, 1976.

Takaki, Ronald. *Strangers from a Different Shore: A History of Asian Americans*. Boston: Little, Brown and Co., 1989.

Taverna, Odette. "Josephine Patrick." *Midweek* (March 11, 1992): 19–21.

Wong, Sau-ling Cynthia. *Reading Asian American Literature: From Necessity to Extravagance*. Princeton: Princeton University Press, 1993.

Stories

Passage into Life

1

Allos was five when he first became aware of the world.

One morning his father sent him to the house of the landlord with a basket of goat meat. He was admitted by a servant who took him into the house. The landlord and his family were having dinner, and when Allos entered the dining room they stopped eating and covered their noses.

"What is in that basket?" asked the landlord.

"Goat meat, sir," Allos said.

"Why did you bring it here?" asked the landlord's wife.

"My father told me to give it to you, Madam," he said.

"Who is your father?" asked the landlord.

"My father works on your land, Your Excellency," Allos said humbly.

"We don't eat goat," shouted the landlord. "Take it away!"

"Peasants! Poor peasants!" sneered one of the landlord's children.

Allos went to the door, weak with shame. He ran out of the yard dragging the basket behind him and shouting to the world that he would never go back to that house again.

2

When Allos was six something happened that definitely changed the course of his life.

He was playing with his dog when he saw Narciso running toward the river. Narciso was his age and a good friend. He stopped playing with the dog and ran after Narciso. He ran swiftly, feeling the earth moving away under him, but every stride he made seemed to push him farther from his friend. When he arrived at the river, Narciso had already jumped naked into the water and was shouting to him.

Allos watched him. Narciso was going downstream. Allos could not understand what was happening. Pausing momentarily at the edge of the high embankment, Allos called to his friend. But at that same instant Narciso's head disappeared under the water.

And then Allos knew.

That evening, when Narciso's body had been found and laid out in a coffin, Allos went into the house silently to see the face of the dead boy for the last time. Tears appeared in his eyes.

Allos suddenly rushed out of the house and ran into the yard where the bright moonlight was shimmering in the guava trees. It was quiet there and for a while he stood crying under a tree, smelling the fragrance of the guavas in bloom. Now a nightingale started singing somewhere in the orchard, followed by another, and still another until the whole yard seemed full of them. He listened, drying his eyes. And when he saw a nightingale singing above his head he began to smile.

And then Allos forgot his dead friend. He burst into a song and started running happily in the moonlight until the trees became white castles sailing on a huge cloud of music.

3

Allos walked behind his mother in the rain. It was his first time to go to the town market. There was a sack of fresh peanuts on his back. His mother carried a big basket of vegetables on her head.

"Are you really going to buy a new straw hat, Mother?" Allos asked.

"Yes, son," his mother said. "And if we sell all the peanuts you are carrying, we will also buy a piece of carabao meat for our family."

Allos walked lightly, dreaming of a new straw hat. The rain stopped when they arrived in the public market. They spread a grass mat on the ground in a corner and put their peanuts and vegetables on it.

But nobody came to their corner. Once a man stopped to cast a glance, then hurriedly walked on to a wineshop. In the late afternoon, when the rain began falling again, Allos and his mother gathered their peanuts and vegetables.

They were the last to leave the public market. And Allos, who realized now that he would not have a straw hat, walked blindly, knowing that this day would never be forgotten as long as he lived.

Oh, Allos, hide in the thorns and thickets of the world!

4

Allos was standing in front of the store when the man came to the door and called to him.

"You like to have one of those candies, son?" he asked.

"Yes, sir," Allos said. He had been standing there for an hour wondering how to get the long red stick of candy. "Yes, sir," he said again.

"Well, son, come inside and mop the floor," said the man.

Allos thought that the man was very nice indeed. Eagerly he swept and mopped and dried the floor of the store. When he had put away all the tools in the closet, the man came out of his office and told Allos to cut the grass in the yard.

Allos found a sickle and a long sharp knife in the kitchen. He bent and knelt, swinging the sickle and the knife. Finally he finished the job. He was standing under a tree and wiping the beads of perspiration off his face when the man came out and told him to haul drinking water form the well.

Allos took the large bucket from the rack on the wall and went to the well. He filled all the drinking jars and cans in the store.

"Good boy," said the man. "Now you can have your stick of candy."

The man found a mouldy candy in a corner of the display case and handed it to the boy. Allos grabbed the candy and ran out. But he was so hungry and tired that the candy made him ill. He threw it away and started running toward home.

He had forgotten to thank the man for being so kind and generous.

5

Now, finally, Allos was going to school. On his way home, carrying a big picture book under his arm, he stopped several times in the street and tried to decipher the big words under the pictures. Somewhere in this big book, he thought, was the magic door to all that he wanted to know.

He walked on, thinking of his seven years. At home, if one of his cousins were present, Allos would ask for his help. But when he reached the gate, Allos saw many people hanging on the fence around the house. There was a wild commotion in the yard, and women were crying hysterically and children were bawling loudly.

Allos ran in the yard to see what was going on. He stopped suddenly when he saw that his father was tied to a tree and one of his brothers was beating him with a stick. His uncle was trying to grab away the stick, but his brother's wife was pulling his uncle by the hair. Farther away, under the house, his mother was rolling in the dust with his brother's oldest daughter.

Allos was aroused. A great fury surged in him. He grabbed a piece of wood and rushed upon his cousin, who was already beating his mother's head with all her fury. He drove his cousin away. Then he rushed upon his brother and started beating his legs and arms. He could not reach his head. His brother turned around and kicked him in his stomach. Allos fell in the dust, but for a moment only. Somewhere he saw a big knife, and he grabbed it, running back to his father's rescue.

Now his brother and uncle were grappling like mad dogs in the dust. He went to his father and cut the ropes that bound him. His father suddenly broke loose and rushed upon the two men who were rolling and grunting. Allos jumped upon them with the knife. But several men jumped over the fence and took the knife away from him.

Allos ran across the yard and into the street. He ran furiously for hours until he could not move any more. He sat down weeping. His agony was beyond consolation. When he became aware of his surroundings night was falling and a few stars were already in the sky. He had wandered far away from home.

Allos walked aimlessly for hours. He stopped to sleep under a tree, but the fear of wild animals made him walk on. He traveled eastward, following the morning star. At last fatigue came upon him, and he lay down beside a stream and went to sleep.

When he woke up the sun was already in the sky. He jumped to his feet, frightened and bewildered. An old farmer was sitting beside him, watching him with amusement.

"Where am I, sir?" Allos asked.

"You are in the village of Batong," said the old man.

"I am far away from home," Allos said.

"And where is that?" asked the old man.

"The village of Togay, sir," he said.

"You are indeed far from home," said the old man. "But you should go home right away. Your parents might be worried about you. Today of all the days of the year is the most significant. Somewhere in this world our Lord, Jesus Christ, is born again. So go home to your parents and rejoice with them."

The old man was so kind, Allos thought. Why was it different at home? But he would go home and ask for forgiveness.

"I don't know how to go home," Allos said finally.

"Well, I have a small cart," said the old man. "It will take you home."

Riding with the old man to his village, Allos knew that he would never forget this man who showed kindness to him.

6

Allos was standing on the corner of his street when he saw several boys stoning a man. He picked up a bamboo stick and ran to the scene.

It was old man Remic. He was covering his head with his hands. One of the older boys hit him on the knee. Remic slowly went down and rolled in the dust.

Allos chased the boys away with his stick. When they were gone he returned to the old man. Remic was already on his feet. He was wiping the blood off his face and legs.

"Thank you, son," Remic told him.

"Why did they stone you, Remic?" Allos asked.

"They think I am crazy," he said. "They think I am all alone in the world."

"You are not crazy, Remic," Allos said. "And you are not alone."

"That is true enough," Remic said. "But they can't understand it. Now it is they who are alone and crazy."

When the old man was gone, Allos picked up the stick again and started running and beating wildly in the wind. He rushed into his yard and grabbed the first tree there and wept silently until his father carried him into the house.

7

Night was falling.

Allos took the carabao from its peg and rode homeward. He was the last herdsboy to leave the pasture. The animal was full and lazy, but it was patient and kind to the boy.

Allos washed the carabao in the river. Then the animal walked slowly in the narrow street, its big stomach swaying and thundering like a drum. When they came to the gate, Allos jumped off the carabao's back and toward his house.

It was dark.

Allos, leaning against the carabao, wondered where his people had gone. They were still there when he left for the pasture that morning. He hugged the animal affectionately, not knowing what to do. And for the first time he felt a great need to hear his people shout and laugh and sing again.

Oh, Allos don't be afraid! The good earth will comfort you in her dark womb!

8

And again the following year, coming home from school, he saw his mother trying to fell a coconut with a long bamboo pole. His mother was short and weak; she gave up after an hour of futile efforts and went back to the house.

Allos found the smallest tree in the yard and climbed it. He was detaching a fruit with one hand and holding tightly on to the trunk with the other when suddenly everything went dark and for a brief moment only he realized that he was falling.

Afterward Allos remembered lying on the ground and the night coming over him. Painfully he rolled over and saw one fruit beside him. Then he knew that he had fallen with it. He crawled toward his house, pushing the coconut slowly with his head. When he came to the ladder, Allos bit the coconut and climbed up step by step. His body was afire and there was a stabbing pain in his head.

Then his mother saw him reaching for the pole on the landing and trying to shove the coconut into the door with his head. His mother shrieked. Allos looked at her for a moment and knew why he had done it, but at the same instant he also ceased to know.

9

Then there was that day when Allos came home and found that all his people were gone. He sat in the kitchen wondering and waiting. When night came he looked into all the pots for something to eat. But they were all empty and clean.

Allos went out of the house and walked to his cousin's house. It was dinner time and his relatives were seated around a small table. There was a steaming boiled chicken and a large platter of pearly white rice on the table. But when his uncle invited him to join them, Allos felt ashamed and forgot his hunger. It was then that he knew how miserable it was to be poor and alone.

Allos went back to his house and boiled some leaves and a handful of grass that he had found in the yard. He ate in the dark knowing that he would never be brave enough to go into the world begging for food or kindness or pity.

10

There was one thing that drove Allos to thinking, and it was watching his mother work all day and half of the night. He knew that his mother woke up at five every morning and started preparing breakfast for the family, and after that, when the members of his family had departed, his mother cleaned the house and washed clothes in the river. At noon, however, she stopped her work and rushed back to the house to prepare lunch, and when this task was performed she returned to the river to finish her washing. Then in the evening, in the midst of the family's laughter, she prepared dinner. When the family was fed, Allos watched his mother clean the dishes and the kitchen. And then, when all the members of the family were in bed except Allos, his mother started ironing the day's washing in the faint lamplight. It was past midnight when he heard his mother creep to her grass mat near the door.

This had been his mother's routine for as long as he could remember. The only variation was when she went to the farm to help his father with the planting and harvesting of rice. Or when she went to the town market to sell a basket of vegetables so that there would be a piece of meat for the family.

Allos often wondered why his mother did not get sick. But one rainy day, carrying a large basket of vegetables, his mother fell under the strain and broke her knee. He helped his mother stumble into the house, running back to the street to pick up the scattered vegetables.

When he returned to the house his mother was writhing with pain. Allos wiped the beads of perspiration off her face, knowing that the world would never again be the same if something fatal happened to his mother.

"I will not believe in God any more if you die, Mother," Allos said.

"Son, little son, you must believe in God always," his mother said.

"Yes, Mother," he said. But Allos knew that he would never believe in God, or in any man, or in himself, if his mother died.

11

Allos was eleven when his older sister came back from the city to live with them. Marcia was a very quiet girl. Allos could not understand it. All the other members of the family were always shouting and laughing and singing. Marcia, however, walked silently in the house and always sat by the window until midnight.

Allos tried to talk to her sometimes, but Marcia only looked at him without saying anything. Her eyes were lifeless when she looked at him.

But one day Allos asked, "Why is my sister Marcia always sitting by the window, Mother?"

"She is waiting for a husband, son," his mother said.

"Is it difficult for her to get a husband?" he asked.

"Yes," his mother answered.

"Why?" Allos wanted to know.

"Because we are poor, son," his mother said finally. "Nobody wants to marry a poor girl."

And Allos, knowing it to be a fact indeed, rushed out of the house wondering why there were poor people. He picked up a stone in the yard and threw it with all his might at a hen that was scratching near the fence. And then he ran furiously down the street and crying to himself that when he grew up he would become rich, but when he reached the river he did not know where to get the money.

Allos plunged into the water hoping that he would die. But several farmers came to his rescue and took him home. When his mother asked him why he did it, Allos looked at her with tears in his eyes.

12

Allos was on his way to church when he saw a big crowd near the wineshop. He rushed to the scene and pushed his way through the crowd of milling men and women. And there in the center was an old man who was bleeding profusely. Several men were beating and kicking him in the face.

Allos was surprised and angry at the same time, because he knew that this old man had been collecting rags and empty bottles for years in his town, but he had never bothered or cheated anyone. He was only an old man who went from house to house buying discarded rags for five centavos per pound and one centavo per empty bottle. He carried a long bamboo pole on his shoulders and at either end hung a basket where he deposited his possessions. The old man usually passed by his house, bent and staggering under his heavy load, and sometimes he stopped near his gate to fan himself with his battered straw hat. He was barefooted and his patched cotton pants were rolled up tightly to his knees so that Allos could see his spindly legs and knotted veins. That was why Allos was sometimes impelled, when he saw the old man staggering with his load, to go out and offer to help him.

But now the men were beating him and kicking his face in the dust. Allos could not understand it so he fell upon the old man's tormentors and tried to push them away.

A man grabbed him, saying, "Keep out of this, son. What have you got to do with him anyway?"

"You are hurting him," Allos cried. "He is a very sick old man."

"He is only a Chinaman," said the man.

Allos had never heard the word before. "What is a Chinaman?" he asked.

"A Chinaman is a foreigner in our country and a spreader of foul diseases among our people," the man told him. "This man is a Chinaman."

"I never saw him spread any diseases," Allos protested.

But the man instructed two of the bigger boys to hold Allos, while he went back to the old man and started beating him again. Allos bit and kicked, but in vain. He looked around pleadingly, but no one tried to help the old man. They stood there and watched him rolling in the dust and even emitted cries of joy when he started to bleed. Finally the old man stopped resisting. He lay still near his broken bottles and burning rags.

The crowd began to disperse quickly. And there was Allos, left with the old man in the approaching night. He knelt in the dust and picked up the old man and blew warmly upon his face. And he wondered as he tried to revive the old man's breath what it was that distinguished him from his people.

"He looks the same," Allos murmured. "He even looks like my father." Then he said fearfully, "Wake up, old man. I will tell you we are the same! Please wake up!"

But the old man was already dead.

13

Allos's father was dying. He heard his mother talking with one of his uncles that if they had money his father had a good chance to live. Suddenly he remembered his rich cousin who had just arrived in town with a big car and a beautiful young wife. He rushed out of the house hoping his cousin would be home and willing to help him.

Allos was entering the gate when he saw his cousin coming down the house with his wife. He was royally dressed and there was a shiny black cane in his hand. His wife was dressed beyond imagination. She was smiling widely and looking at the world like a papaya in bloom.

Allos stopped for a moment, wondering how two creatures could be endowed with so much good fortune. And then bravely he rushed toward his cousin, almost colliding into him. But his cousin brushed him away with his cane, away from his immaculate suit and beautiful young wife, and suddenly, Allos felt, away from his only hope and into the dark well of his shame.

His cousin did not even talk to him. When he and his wife were comfortably seated in the car, he opened the window and threw a dime in Allos's direction. And then they drove away.

Allos picked up the small silver dime and looked at it for a long time.

14

Allos was fourteen when he met the stranger. He was wandering aimlessly in the dry river when he saw him. The stranger was lying quietly on the sand. Allos sat beside him.

"Don't be sad, son," said the stranger.

"How did you know I am sad?" Allos asked.

"I know," said the stranger.

Allos did not understand what the stranger meant, but he said, "I have no more father. He died today."

"I'm sorry to hear that, son," said the stranger. "But it is like this with all of us in the world: No one is really an orphan as long as there is another man living. As long as there is one man living and working and thinking on the earth."

"I don't know," Allos said. "I had a very good father. He had worked all his life and when there was not enough to eat in the house he would give up his own portion and offer it to me. I don't know if there is a father like him in the whole world."

"I suppose not," said the stranger. "I had a father, too. And he was a very good father. But he died like your father. Death is not a bad thing. It is only the beginning of a much longer life. It is the beginning of a life that never ends. All your dreams, all the things that you want to do in this world but can't achieve—well, you'll have them all in that other place. And more than that, son. Your father will be waiting for you when you arrive. All your other relatives will be there too waiting for your homecoming. Yes, that is the home for us all."

"I didn't know that, sir," Allos said finally. "I thought that death is the end of everything."

"You are wrong, son," said the stranger. "Now come with me and I'll show you that you are wrong."

They got up together and crossed the river and walked through a wide valley. They walked on for two days and two nights, stopping now and then to see the land around them. And then on the third day they came to a tall mountain and climbed upward until they reached the top. But it was night again and it was very quiet all around them.

There on the other side of the mountain was an impenetrable darkness, and a silence that had no voice. Allos looked and knew at last that there was a life without end.

He turned to the stranger, saying, "Yes, it is all true . . ."

15

Allos watched the stranger walk down the mountain to the other side until he was swallowed by the darkness. He was left alone in the night, but felt that he could contend with whatever would befall him.

He turned back and started to descend toward the valley where he had come from, toward home and his people. When he had crossed the last mountain that divided his land and the unknown country where the stranger had disappeared, Allos stood on the highest peak and watched with a mounting joy the dazzling brilliance of the new sun shining above all his rivers and plains.

Now Allos knew: there in the known world he must go to seek a new life, seek it among the living until he would have enough time to pause and ponder on the mystery of the dead. And so with light steps he walked toward his valley, a song of joy warming his whole being until it became the song of all his living dreams.

The Story of a Letter

When my brother Berto was thirteen he ran away from home and went to Manila. We did not hear from him until eight years later, and he was by that time working in a little town in California. He wrote a letter in English, but we could not read it. Father carried it in his pocket all summer, hoping the priest in our village would read it for him.

The summer ended gloriously and our work on the farm was done. We gathered firewood and cut grass on the hillsides for our animals. The heavy rains came when we were patching up the walls of our house. Father and I wore palm overcoats and worked in the mud, rubbing vinegar on our foreheads and throwing it around us to keep the lightning away. The rains ceased suddenly, but the muddy water came down from the mountains and flooded the river.

We made a bamboo raft and floated slowly along the water. Father sat in the center of the raft and took the letter from his pocket. He looked at it for a long time, as though he were committing it to memory. When we reached the village church it was midnight, but there were many people in the yard. We tied our raft to the riverbank and dried our clothes on the grass.

A woman came and told us that the priest had died of overeating at a wedding. Father took our clothes off the grass and we put them on. We untied our raft and rowed against the slow currents back to our house. Father was compelled to carry the letter for another year, waiting for the time when my brother Nicasio would come home from school. He was the only one in our family who could read and write.

When the students returned from the cities, Father and I went to town with a sack of peanuts. We stood under the arbor tree in the station and watched every bus that stopped. He heated a pile of dry sand with burning stones and roasted peanuts. At night we sat in the coffee shop and talked with the loafers and gamblers. Then the last students arrived, but my brother Nicasio was not with them. We gave up waiting and went back to the village.

When summer came again we plowed the land and planted corn. Then we were informed that my brother Nicasio had gone to America. Father was greatly disappointed. He took the letter of my brother Berto from his pocket and locked it in a small box. We put our minds on our work and after two years the letter was forgotten.

Toward the end of my ninth year, a tubercular young man appeared in our village. He wanted to start a school for the children and the men were enthusiastic. The drummer went around the village and announced the good news. The farmers gathered in a vacant lot not far from the cemetery and started building a schoolhouse. They shouted at one another with joy and laughed aloud. The wind carried their laughter through the village.

I saw them at night lifting the grass roof on their shoulders. I ran across the fields and stood by the well, watching them place the rafters on the long bamboo posts. The men were stripped to the waist and their cotton trousers were rolled up to their thighs. The women came with their earthen jars and hauled drinking water, pausing in the clear moonlight to watch the men with secret joy.

Then the schoolhouse was finished. I heard the bell ring joyfully in the village. I ran to the window and saw boys and girls going to school. I saw Father on our carabao, riding off toward our house. I took my straw hat off the wall and rushed to the gate.

Father bent down and reached for my hands. I sat behind him on the bare back of the animal. The children shouted and slapped their bellies. When we reached the school yard the carabao stopped without warning. Father fell to the ground and rolled into the well, screaming aloud when he touched the water. I grabbed the animal's tail and hung on to it till it rolled on its back in the dust.

I rushed to the well and lowered the wooden bucket. I tied the rope to the post and shouted for help. Father climbed slowly up the rope to the mouth of the well. The bigger boys came down and helped me pull Father out. He stood in the sun and shook the water off his body. He told me to go into the schoolhouse with the other children.

We waited for the teacher to come. Father followed me inside and sat on a bench behind me. When the teacher arrived we stood as one person and waited for him to be seated. Father came to my bench and sat quietly for a long time. The teacher started talking in our dialect, but he talked so fast we could hardly understand him.

When he distributed some little Spanish books, Father got up and asked what language we would learn. The teacher told us that it was Spanish. Father asked him if he knew English. He said he knew only Spanish and our dialect. Father took my hand and we went out of the schoolhouse. We rode the carabao back to our house.

Father was disappointed. He had been carrying my brother's letter for almost three years now. It was still unread. The suspense was hurting him and me, too. It was the only letter he had received in all the years that I had known him, except some letters that came from the government once a year asking him to pay his taxes.

When the rains ceased, a strong typhoon came from the north and swept away the schoolhouse. The teacher gave up teaching and married a village girl. Then he took up farming and after two years his wife gave birth to twins. The men in the village never built a schoolhouse again.

I grew up suddenly and the desire to see other places grew. It moved me like a flood. It was impossible to walk a kilometer away from our house without wanting to run away to the city. I tried to run away a few times, but whenever I reached the town, the farm always called me back. I could not leave Father because he was getting old.

Then our farm was taken away from us. I decided to go to town for a while and live with Mother and my two little sisters. Father remained in the village. He came to town once with a sack of wild tomatoes and bananas. But the village called him back again.

I left our town and traveled to other places. I went to Baguio in the northern part of the Philippines and worked in the marketplace posing naked for American tourists who seemed to enjoy the shameless nudity of the natives. An American woman, who claimed that she had come from Texas, took me to Manila.

She was a romantic painter. When we arrived in the capital she rented a nice large house where the sun was always shining. There were no children of my age. There were men and women who never smiled. They spoke through their noses. The painter from Texas asked me to undress every morning; she worked industriously. I had never dreamed of making a living by exposing my body to a stranger. That experience made me roar with laughter for many years.

One time, while I was still in the woman's house, I remembered the wide ditch near our house in the village where the young girls used to take a bath in the nude. A cousin of mine stole the girls' clothes and then screamed behind some bushes. The girls ran about with their hands between their legs. I thought of this incident when I felt shy, hiding my body with my hands from the woman painter. When I had saved a little money I took a boat for America.

I forgot my village for a while. When I went to a hospital and lay in bed for two years, I started to read books with hunger. My reading was started by a nurse who thought I had come from China. I lied to her without thinking of it, but I told a good lie. I had no opportunity to learn when I was outside in the world but the security and warmth of the hospital gave it to me. I languished in bed for two years with great pleasure. I was no longer afraid to live in a strange world and among strange peoples.

Then at the end of the first year, I remembered the letter of my brother Berto. I crept out of bed and went to the bathroom. I wrote a letter to Father asking him to send the letter to me for translation. I wanted to translate it, so that it would be easy for him to find a man in our village to read it to him.

The letter arrived six months later. I translated it into our dialect and sent it back with the original. I was now better. The doctors told me that I could go out of the hospital. I used to stand by the window for hours asking myself why I had forgotten to laugh in America. I was afraid to go out into the world. I had been confined too long, I had forgotten what it was like on the outside.

I had been brought to the convalescent ward when the Civil War in Spain started some three years before. Now, after the peasants' and workers' government was crushed, I was physically ready to go out into the world and start a new life. There was some indignation against fascism in all civilized lands. To most of us, however, it was the end of a great cause.

I stood at the gate of the hospital, hesitating. Finally, I closed my eyes and walked into the city. I wandered all over Los Angeles for some time, looking for my brothers. They had been separated from me since childhood. We had had, separately and together, a bitter fight for existence. I had heard that my brother Nicasio was in Santa Barbara, where he was attending college. Berto, who never stayed in one place for more than three months at a time, was rumored to be in Bakersfield waiting for the grape season.

I packed my suitcase and took a bus to Santa Barbara. I did not find my brother there. I went to Bakersfield and wandered in the streets asking for my brother. I went to Chinatown and stood in line for the free chop-suey that was served in the gambling houses to the loafers and gamblers. I could not find my brother in either town. I went to the vineyards looking for him. I was convinced that he was not in that valley. I took a bus for Seattle.

The hiring halls were full of men waiting to be shipped to the canneries in Alaska. I went to the dance halls and poolrooms. But I could not find my brothers. I took the last boat to Alaska and worked there for three months. I wanted to save money so that I could have something to spend when I returned to the mainland.

When I came back to the West Coast, I took a bus to Portland. Beyond Tacoma, near the district where Indians used to force the hop pickers into marriage, I looked out the window and saw my brother Berto in a beer tavern. I knew it was my brother although I had not seen him for many years. There was something in the way he had turned his head toward the bus that made me think I was right. I stopped at the next town and took another bus back to Tacoma. But he was already gone.

I took another bus and went to California. I stopped in Delano. The grape season was in full swing. There were many workers in town. I stood in the poolrooms and watched the players. I went to a beer place and sat in a booth. I ordered several bottles and thought long and hard of my life in America.

Toward midnight a man in a big overcoat came in and sat beside me. I asked him to drink beer with me without looking at his face. We started drinking together and then, suddenly, I saw a familiar face in the dirty mirror on the wall. I almost screamed. He was my brother

Nicasio—but he had grown old and emaciated. We went outside and walked to my hotel.

The landlord met me with a letter from the Philippines. In my room I found that my letter to Father, when I was in the hospital, and the translation of my brother Berto's letter to him, had been returned to me. It was the strangest thing that had ever happened. I had never lived in Delano before. I had never given my forwarding address to anybody. The letter was addressed to me at a hotel I have never seen before.

It was now ten years since my brother Berto had written the letter to Father. It was eighteen years since he had run away from home. I stood in the center of my room and opened it. The note attached to it said that Father had died some years before. It was signed by the postmaster of my town.

I bent down and read the letter—the letter that had driven me away from my village and had sent me half-way around the world—read it the very day a letter came from the government telling that my brother Berto was already serving in the Navy—and the same day that my brother Nicasio was waiting to be inducted into the Army. I held the letter in my hand, and suddenly, I started to laugh—choking with tears at the mystery and wonder of it all.

> "Dear Father [my brother wrote]:
> America is a great country. Tall buildings. Wide good land. The people walking. But I feel sad. I am writing you this hour of my sentimental.
>
> Your son—Berto."

Be American

It was not Consorcio's fault. My cousin was an illiterate peasant from the vast plains of Luzon. When he came off the boat in San Francisco, he could neither read nor write English or Ilocano, our dialect. I met him when he arrived, and right away he had bright ideas in his head.

"Cousin, I want to be American," he told me.

"Good," I said. "That is the right thing to do. But you have plenty of time. You are planning to live permanently in the United States, are you not?"

"Sure, cousin," he said. "But I want to be American right away. On the boat I say, 'Consorcio stoody Engleesh right away.' Good ideeyas, eh, cousin?"

"It is," I said. "But the first thing for you to do is look for a job."

"Sure, cousin. You have joob for me?"

I did. I took him to a countryman of ours who owned a small restaurant on Kearny Street. He had not done any dishwashing in the Philippines, so he broke a few dishes before he realized that the dishes were not coconut shells that he could flagrantly throw around the place, the way he used to do in his village where coconut shells were plates and carved trunks of trees were platters and his fingers were spoons. He had never seen bread and butter before, so he lost some weight before he realized that he had to eat these basic things like the rest of us, and be an American, which was his own idea in the first place. He had never slept in a bed with a mattress before, so he had to suffer from severe cold before he realized that he had to sleep inside the bed, under the blankets, but not on top of the spread, which was what he had done during his first two weeks in America. And of course he had never worn shoes before, so he had to suffer a few blisters on both feet before he realized that he had to walk lightfooted, easy, and even graceful, but not the way he used to do it in his village, which was like wrestling with a carabao or goat.

All these natural things he had to learn during his first two weeks. But he talked about his Americanization with great confidence.

"You see, cousin," he told me, "I have earned mony quick. I poot the hoot dashes in the sink, wash-wash, day come, day out, week gone—mony! Simple?"

"Fine," I said.

"You know what I done with mony?"

"No."

"I spent all."

"On what?"

"Books. Come see my room."

I went with him to his small room at the back of the restaurant where he was working, near the washrooms. And sure enough, he had lined the four walls of his room with big books. I looked at the titles. He had a cheap edition of the classics, books on science, law and mathematics. He even had some brochures on political and governmental matters. All were books that a student or even a professor would take time to read.

I turned to my cousin. He was smiling with pride.

"Well, I hope these big books will make you an American faster," I told him.

"Sure, cousin. How long I wait?"

"Five years."

"Five years?" There was genuine surprise in his dark peasant face. "Too long. I do not wait. I make faster—one year."

"It is the law," I assured him.

"No good law. One year enough for Consorcio. He make good American citizen."

"There is nothing you can do about it."

"I change law."

"Go ahead."

"You see, cousin."

But he was puzzled. So I left him. I left San Francisco. When I saw him a year later, he was no longer washing dishes. But he still had the pardonable naivete of a peasant from the plains of Luzon.

"Where are you working now?" I asked him.

"Bakery," he said. "I make da bread. I make da donot. I made da pys."

"Where?"

"Come, cousin, I show you."

It was a small shop, a three-man affair. Consorcio was the handyboy in the place scrubbing the floor, washing the pots and pans; and he was also the messenger. The owner was the baker, while his wife was the saleswoman. My cousin lived at the back of the building, near the washrooms. He had a cot in a corner of the dark room. But the books were gone.

"What happened to your books?" I asked him.

He looked sad. Then he said, "I sold, cousin."

"Why?"

"I cannot read. I cannot understand. Words too big and too long."

"You should begin with the simple grammar books."

"Those cannot read also. What to do now, cousin?"

"You still want to be an American citizen?"

"Sure."

"Go to night school."

"Is a place like that?"

"Yes."

"No use, cousin, no money."

"The school is free." I told him. "It is for foreign-born people. For adults, so they could study American history."

"Free? I go now."

"The school opens only at night."

"I work night."

"Well, work in the daytime. Look for another job. You still want to be an American, don't you?"

"Sure, but I like boss-man. What to do?"

"Tell him the truth."

"You help me?"

I did. We went to the boss-man. I explained the matter as truthfully as I could and he understood Consorcio's problems. But he asked me to find someone to take the place of my cousin's place, which I did too, so we shook hands around and departed in the best of humor. I helped

Consorcio register at the night school, [and] looked for another job for him as a janitor in an apartment building. Then I left him, wishing him the best of luck.

I worked in Alaska the next two years. When I returned to the mainland, I made it my duty to pass through San Francisco. But my cousin had left his janitor job and the night school. I could not find his new address, and it seemed that no one knew him well enough in the Filipino community.

I did not think much of his disappearance because we are a wandering people due to the nature of our lowly occupations, which take us from place to place, following the seasons. When I received a box of grapes from a friend, I knew he was working in the grape fields in either Fresno or Delano, depending on the freight mark. When I received a box of asparagus, I knew he was working in Stockton. But when it was a crate of lettuce, he was working in Santa Maria or Salinas, depending on the freight mark again. And in the summertime when I received a large barrel of salmon, I knew he was working the salmon canneries in Alaska. There were no letters, no post cards—nothing. But these surprising boxes, crates and barrels that arrived periodically were the best letters in the world. What they contained were lovingly distributed among my city friends. Similarly, when I was in one of my own wanderings, which were done in cities and large towns, I sent my friend or friends unsealed envelopes bursting with the colored pictures of actresses and other beautiful women. I addressed these gifts to poolrooms and restaurants in towns where my friends had lived or worked for a season, because they were bound to go to any of these havens of the homeless wanderer. However, when another curious wanderer opened the envelopes and pilfered the pictures, it was not a crime. The enjoyment which was originally intended for my friends was his and his friends. That is the law of the nomad: finders keepers.

But Consorcio had not yet learned the unwritten law of the nomad. I did not expect him to send me boxes, crates, and barrels from faraway Alaska. So I did not know where I could locate him.

I wandered in and out of Los Angeles the next two years. At the beginning of the third year, when I was talking to the sleeping birds in Pershing Square, I felt a light hand on my shoulders. I was not usually curious about hands, but it was well after midnight and the cops were wandering in and out of the place. So I turned around—and found Consorcio.

I found a new Consorcio. He had aged and the peasant naivete was gone from his face. In his eyes was now a hidden fear. His hands danced and flew when he was talking, and even when he was not talking, as though he were slapping the wind with both hands or clapping with one hand. Have you ever heard the noise of one hand clapping?

That was Consorcio, after five years in America. He was either slapping the wind with both hands or clapping with one hand. So I guided him out of the dark park to a lighted place, where we had coffee until the city awoke to give us another day of hope. Of course, I sat in silence for a long time because it was the fear of deep silence. And Consorcio sat for a long time too, because by now he had learned to hide in the deep silence that was flung like a mourning cloak across the face of the land. When we talked our sentences were short and punctuated by long silences. So we conversed somewhat like this:

"Been wandering everywhere."

"No job."

"Nothing anywhere."

"Where have you been all three years?"

Silence.

"No finished school?"

Silence.

"Not American citizen yet?"

"You should have told me."

"Told you what?"

"Filipinos can't become American citizens."

"Well, I could have told you. But I wanted you to learn."

"At least I speak better English now."

"This is a country of great opportunity."

Silence.

"No work?"

"No work."

"How long?"

"I have forgotten."

"Better times will come."

"You have a wonderful dream, cousin," he told me and left. He left Los Angeles for a long time. Then two years later, I received a crate of oranges from him. The freight mark was San Jose. Now I knew he was working and had learned the unwritten law of the wanderers on this troubled earth. So as I ate the oranges, I recalled his last statement: You have a wonderful dream, cousin . . .

I had a wonderful dream. But I dreamed it for both of us, for many of us who wandered in silence.

Then the boxes and crates became more frequent. Then a barrel of salmon came from Alaska. And finally, the letters came. My cousin Consorcio, the one-time illiterate peasant from the vast plains of Luzon, had indeed become an American without knowing it. His letters were full of wondering and pondering about many things in America. How he realized his naivete when he had landed in San Francisco. But he realized also that he could not ask too much in a strange land. And it was this realization that liberated him from his peasant prison, his heritage, and eventually led him to a kind of work to which he dedicated his time and life until the end.

I was in Oregon when I received a newspaper from Consorcio, postmarked Pismo Beach. It was the first issue of his publication for agricultural workers in California. It was in English. From then on, I received all issues of his publication. For five years it existed defending the workers and upholding the rights and liberties of all Americans, native or foreign born, so that, as he began to understand the nature of American society, he became more belligerent in his editorials and had to go to jail a few times for his ideas about freedom and peace.

Yes, indeed Consorcio: you have become an American, a real American. And this land that we have known too well is not yet denuded by the rapacity of men. Rolling like a beautiful woman with an overflowing abundance of fecundity and murmurous with her eternal mystery, there she lies before us like a great mother. To her we always return from our prodigal wanderings and searchings for an anchorage in the sea of life; from her we always draw our sustenance and noble thoughts, to add to her glorious history.

But the war came. And war ended Consorcio's newspaper work and his crusade for a better America. And it ended his life also. When he was brought back from overseas, he knew he would not last long. But he talked the way he had written his editorials, measured sentences that rang like music, great poetry, and soft, soft. He would not shed a tear; but his heart must have been crying, seeing eternal darkness coming toward him, deep, deep in the night of perpetual sleep. Yes he would not shed a tear; but he must have been crying, seeing that there was so much to do with so little time left. There was in his voice a kindness for me—unhappy, perhaps, that he could not impart what he had learned from his wanderings on this earth; unhappy, also, because he knew that it would take all the people to unmake the unhappiness which had caught up with us. And now, fifteen years after his arrival in San Francisco, he was dying.

And he died. But at least he received his most cherished dream: American citizenship. He did realize later that he had become an American before he received his papers, when he began to think and write lovingly about *our* America. He gave up many things, and finally his own life, to realize his dream.

But Consorcio is not truly dead. He lives again in my undying love for the American earth. And soon, when I see the last winter coming to the last leaf, I will be warm with the thought that another wanderer shall inherit the wonderful dream which my cousin and I had dreamed and tried to realize in America.

The Soldier

They were arguing in the living room.

"You've invited him to come here?" the mother asked.

"Why not?" the daughter said. "He's nice and intelligent."

The mother looked at her daughter with horror. "A soldier?" she said. "A Filipino soldier?"

The father came from the kitchen with a glass of wine in one hand and a bottle in the other.

He had heard his wife and daughter arguing when he came home, but had gone straight to his room as though he were unconcerned. At the dinner table his wife and daughter had been very solemn. At the end of the dinner his wife had looked strangely at the girl. The daughter had rushed to the living room where she threw herself into a chair. He had looked at his wife then, long, questioning her purpose. Their argument had already touched him. He had looked at his wife, through the years of their life together, trying to put his thoughts together.

"Would you like your daughter to bring a Filipino here?" she had asked him.

He had merely looked at her with the great patience of a husband who had worked dutifully for years to have a decent home.

"Would you?" she had cried.

He had walked to the living room without answering her. He had stood near the chair where the girl was weeping. He had wanted to understand her. He had bent over to touch her, but suddenly he had straightened up, stood for a while, eager, then walked to the kitchen for the bottle of wine.

Now, he came out of the kitchen with a glass of wine in one hand, the bottle in the other.

"Go up to your room, Marcella," he said.

The girl looked up at her father the way she had always looked at him when she had pleaded for understanding. All through the years she had always looked at him that way. There was a time when she had come home from school and cried to him. It seemed that she had met a boy that time. If it were not for him, she would have neglected her studies that year.

She looked now at her father as though all the years were crowding in upon her, challenging his victories and deep convictions. He could see in her eyes the light of other years, the strong light that once glowed warmly in his eyes; the immortal light that has shone in other lands and times.

If only I could go back to the beginning, he thought. Instead he said to his daughter, "Go up to your room now, Marcella."

She knew that she was defeated. She jumped from the chair and fled across the room and rushed up the stairway. She slammed the door and flung herself upon the bed, sobbing and kicking the air.

Martha," he said to his wife, looking up the stairs. "Where did she meet him?"

"In the public library."

He walked to his chair and sat down. "Well, he must be a nice boy."

"Walter!" she cried with horror.

He made a motion to go to her, hesitated, sat back and shook his head. Then he got up and walked to the table for his pipe. Suddenly, the doorbell rang out loud.

"That's probably him now," he said.

She brushed the tears from her eyes. The bell rang again. The man walked to the door and opened it. A Filipino soldier was standing in the light rain. He was holding a box of candies.

"Is this Miss Marcella Roberts' home?" he asked.

"Yes," the man said, hesitant, pondering. Then he said, "Come on in."

The soldier walked into the house and stood on the threshold for a moment, the cold of the night outside still clinging heavily to him. The man closed the door and took the soldier's cap, walking over to the far corner of the room where his wife was waiting.

"You are Marcella's mother?" the soldier asked.

"Yes," she said.

"I thought so," the soldier said. "You look exactly as I thought you would, only you are much younger."

"Where is your station?" the man asked.

"Fort Ord," the soldier said.

"How is it out there?"

"It is great," he said. "Nice bunch of fellows in that camp. I like the place. I've been studying seriously."

The man was still standing before the soldier, fumbling deliberately with his pipe.

"I was in the first war—" he started and stopped.

There was a sudden interest in the young man's voice. "Were you?" he said, jumping to his feet.

"I've served ten months in France."

"Then you understand the feelings of a soldier. They say the other war was fought for democracy. Some of those who fought in it say it's a lie. I don't interpret it that way though. It was fought for democracy all right, but somewhere the ideals were gobbled up by powerful men."

The man was beginning to feel that he had something in common with the soldier. The only difference was that, when he was a soldier, he did not have the chance to clarify his beliefs. He was glad that at last, some twenty-five years later, he had met another soldier who, though born in another part of the world, could have been himself, bringing with him the bright hopes he had fought for in that other war.

He walked back to his chair and sat down, facing the soldier. He glanced at his wife swiftly. Looking back at the soldier, a yearning to confide something personal surged through him.

"Have you ever lived in this city before?" he asked.

"Yes," the soldier said. "Ten years ago. But most of the people I knew are gone. This afternoon I walked around looking at the new stores and buildings. I stopped at the newsstands and touched the magazines and newspapers. I like this city very much indeed. Life reacts itself in the city streets. Ten years ago I used to stand in the station watching the people, and always there was a powerful yearning in me to go away. 'Someday,' I used to say to myself, 'I'll go away and never come back.' But I never went away. I remember when I was a little boy my father and I used to go to the mountains just for the sheer joy of walking long distances. I'm like my father, who had a yearning for far away places. It took a war to take me away, though. I might not come back to all this wonderful—" He stopped and looked around the house with a strange affection and sincerity, as though he was storing up the bright image of the room in his mental world. He appreciated all of it.

The man stirred in his chair. "Marcella is ill and she can't come down," he said.

"Ill?" the soldier said, frightened.

"She has the flu, but she'll be all right."

"I hope she'll be all right."

"We'll tell her that you called," the mother said.

"Thank you, Mrs. Roberts," he said. He walked across the room and put the book and box of candies on the table. "I'll leave these candies for Marcella. This small book of poems is written by a Filipino who lived in this city. He was the first of my people to write a book in English."

The man felt the strong pride in the soldier's voice. "We'll give them to her," he said.

"Tell her to get well soon," the soldier said. "Tell her not to get the flu any more. Tell her the weather is dangerous this year." He walked to the door and the man followed him.

"Good night, Mrs. Roberts," he said, and stepped out of the house.

"I'll walk with you to the street," the man said.

The rain had stopped falling and there was a misty moonlight in the trees. There was a fresh smell in the air. The man and the soldier stood in the street, under a wide arc of light.

"What you've said there," the man said with feeling, "is what I've always wanted to say."

"I'm glad you feel that way, sir," the soldier said.

The man gave his hand eagerly. "Good luck, young man," he said.

The Filipino soldier walked into the night. He did not look back to see that the man was watching him walking away.

As Long as the Grass Shall Grow

In the middle of that year when we were picking peas on the hillside, I noticed the school children playing with their teacher in the sun. It was my first time to see her, a young woman of about twenty-five with brown hair and a white dress spotted with blue. The blue sky seemed to absorb the white color of her dress, but from where I stood she appeared all clothed with light blue. The blueness of the sea at the back of the schoolhouse also enhanced the blue dots of her dress. But my eyes were familiar with the bright colors on the hillside, the yellowing leaves of the peas, the sprouting green blades of the summer grass, the royal white crowns of the edelweiss, and the tall gray mountains in the distance, and the silent blue sea below the clear sky.

I had arrived in America, the new land, three months before and had come to this farming town to join friends who had years ago left the Philippines. I had come in time to pick the summer peas. I had been working for over a month now with a crew of young Filipino immigrants who followed the crops and the seasons. At night when our work was done, and we had all eaten and scrubbed the dirt off our bodies, I joined them in dress suit and went to town to shoot pool at a familiar place. I observed that the older men went to the back of the poolroom and played cards all night long. In the morning they went to the field sleepily and talked about their losses and winnings all day. They seemed a bunch of contented workers, but they were actually restless and had no plans for the future.

Then I saw the children. They reminded me of a vanished time. I used to stop at my work and watch them singing and running and screaming in the sun. One dark-haired boy in particular, about eight, brought back acute memories of a childhood friend who died a violent death when I was ten. We had gone to the fields across the river that afternoon to fly our kites because it was summertime and the breeze was just strong enough to carry our playthings to high altitudes.

Suddenly, in the midst of our sport, a ferocious carabao broke loose from its peg and came plunging wildly after us, trapping my friend and goring him to death. That night when I went to see him, and realized that he was truly dead, I ran out of the house and hid in the back yard where the moonlight was like a silver column in the guava trees. I stood sobbing under a guava, smelling the sweetness of the papaya blossoms in the air. Then suddenly nightingales burst into a glorious song. I stopped crying and listened to them. Gradually I became vaguely comforted and could accept the fact that my friend would not come back to life again. I gathered an armful of papaya blossoms and went back into the house and spread them over the coffin. I returned to the guava grove and listened to the nightingales sing all night long.

So this dark-haired boy in a land faraway, many years afterward, stirred a curiosity for the unknown in me that had been dimmed by time. I walked to the schoolhouse one morning and stood by the fence. The children ran to me, as if they knew me. I can't now remember my exact feeling when they reached out their little hands to me. But I know that I suddenly started gathering the red and yellow poppies growing abundantly on the hillside. Then the teacher came out on the porch and called the children back to their classes.

I returned to my work, watching the schoolhouse. In the early afternoon when the children had gone home, I saw the teacher walking toward the hill. She came to me.

"Were you the boy that was at the schoolhouse this morning?" she asked.

"Yes, ma'am," I said.

"How old are you?"

I told her. She looked for a moment toward my companions, who had all stopped working to listen to her.

"You are too young to be working," she said finally. "How far have you gone in school?"

I was ashamed to admit it, but I said: "Third grade, ma'am."

"Would you like to do some reading under me?"

"I'd love to, ma'am," I said softly. I looked at my companions from the corners of my eyes because they would ridicule me if they knew that I wanted some education. I never saw any reading material at our bunkhouse except the semi-nude pictures of women in movie magazines. "I'd love to study some, ma'am," I said. "But I can read only a few words."

"Well, I'll teach you," she said. "What time do you go home?"

"Six o'clock ma'am," I said.

She said, "I'll be at your bunkhouse at eight. That will give you two hours for dinner and a bath. Tell your friends to be ready, too."

"Yes, ma'am," I said. "I will tell them. Some of them went to high school in the Islands, but most of us stopped in the primary grades."

"I'll teach those who are willing," she said. "So be ready at eight sharp."

I watched her walk slowly down the hill. When she reached the highway at the foot of the hill, I waved my hand at her. She waved back and walked on. She drove away in her car, and when she was gone, I went on working quietly. But my companions taunted me. Some of them even implied certain dark things that made me stop picking peas and look at them with a challenge in my eyes. When they finally stopped shouting at me, I resumed my work thinking of some books I would like to read.

The teacher came at the appointed time. She had put on a pair of corduroy pants and an unpressed blue shirt. It was my first time to see a woman dressed like a man. I stole glances at her every time she turned her face away. She brought a story book about ancient times which she read slowly to me. But I was disappointed because my companions did not want to study with me. I noticed that five stayed home and played poker; the others went to town to shoot pool. There was one in the kitchen who kept playing his guitar, stopping only now and then to listen to what we were reading. About ten o'clock in the evening the teacher closed the book and prepared to go. I took her to the door and looked outside where the moon was shining brightly. The grass on the hill was beautiful, and the calm sea farther away was like a polished mirror, and the tall mountains in the horizon were like castles.

"Shall I walk you to the road, ma'am?" I asked.

"Thank you," she said. "I love to walk in the moonlight."

When she was at the gate, I ran after her.

"What is your name, ma'am?" I asked.

"Helen O'Reilly," she said. "Goodnight."

I watched her walk away. She stopped under the tall eucalyptus trees on the highway and looked around the wide silence. After a while she lighted a cigarette and climbed into her car.

Miss O'Reilly came to our bunkhouse every evening after that night. She read stories of long ago, and pages from the history of many nations. My companions slowly joined our course and in two weeks only three of the whole crew stayed away. She took a great interest in her work. After a while she started talking about herself and the town where she had come from and about her people. She was born in a little town somewhere in the Northwest. She had come from a poor family and supported herself through college. Before she graduated the depression came. When she was offered a teaching job in a rural community in California, she accepted it, thinking that she could go on with her studies when she had saved enough money.

Miss O'Reilly was a good teacher. We started giving her peas and flowers that we picked on the hillside when we were working. Once we thought of buying her a dress, but one of the older men said that was improper. So we put the money in a large envelope and gave it to her when she came one evening. She did not want to accept it, but we said that it was a token of our gratitude. She took it then, and when she came again she showed us a gabardine suit that she had bought with it.

We were all very happy then. On the hillside, when we were picking peas, we sometimes stopped and considered the possibility of giving her a party at our bunkhouse. But one evening she came to tell us that some organization in town had questioned her coming to our bunk-house. She told us to go to the schoolhouse when our work was done and study there like regular pupils.

I could not understand why any organization would forbid her to work where she pleased. I was too newly arrived from the islands, too sheltered within my group of fellow Filipinos to have learned the taboos of the mainland, to have seen the American doors shut against us. But I went to the schoolhouse every night with my companions and started writing short sentences on the blackboard. I stood there and looked out of the window. I saw the silent sea and the wide clear sky. Suddenly I wrote a poem about what I saw outside in the night. Miss O'Reilly started laughing because my lines were all wrong and many of the words were misspelled and incorrectly used.

"Now, now," Miss O'Reilly said behind my back, "it's too soon for you to write poetry. We will come to that later."

I blushed.

"What made you do it?" she asked.

"I don't know, Miss O'Reilly," I said.

"Did you ever read poetry before?"

"No, Miss O'Reilly," I said. "I didn't even know it was poetry."

She looked at me with some doubt. Then she went to her table and started reading from the Bible. It was the Song of Solomon. I liked the rich language, the beautiful imagery, and the depth of the old man's passion for the girl and the vineyard.

"This is the best poetry in the world," Miss O'Reilly said when she finished the chapter. "I would like you to remember it. There was a time when men loved deeply and were not afraid to love."

I was touched by the songs. I thought of the pea vines on the hillside and the silent blue sea not far away. And I said to myself: *Some day I will come back in memory to this place and time and write about you, Miss O'Reilly. How gratifying it will be to come back to you with a book in my hands about all that we are feeling here tonight!*

Miss O'Reilly shoved the Bible into my pocket that night. I read it over and over. I read all the school books also. I was beginning to think that when I could save enough money I would live in another town and go to school. But we still had the peas to pick, after that the tomatoes on the other side of the hill.

Then Miss O'Reilly told us she was forbidden by the school board to use the building at night. The directive was for us, of course. Miss O'Reilly did not tell us that, but some of my companions knew what it was all about. When she invited us to go to her boarding house, only a few of us went.

"Come one by one in the dark," she advised us. "And go up the steps very quietly."

"All right, Miss O'Reilly," I said.

So we went to her room at night where we read softly. She told us that there was a sick old woman in the house. One night a man knocked on the door and asked Miss O'Reilly to step out in the hallway for a moment. When Miss O'Reilly came back to the room, I saw that she was perturbed. She looked at us in a maternal way and then toward the hallway with a forgiving look. We resumed our reading, and at our departure Miss O'Reilly told us not to mind anything.

I went again the following night. But I was alone. My companions dropped out. Miss O'Reilly seemed about to tell me something, but she let it drop. I forgot about her uneasiness as we read to each other, but when I left and she accompanied me to the door, she turned suddenly and ran to her room. I thought she had forgotten to give me something, but when her lights went out I went on my way.

I had gone two blocks away when four men approached me in the dark street. Two of them grabbed me and pushed me into a car. Then they drove me for several blocks, turned to a field of carrots, and stopped under a high water tank. They got out of the car and started beating me.

I tried to defend myself, but they were so many. When I had a chance, however, I started to run away, but a man jumped into the car and drove after me. I fell down when the car struck me. They all came and started beating me again. I could not fight back any more. I rolled on my stomach when they kicked me. Once, when I was losing consciousness, I felt the hard heel of a shoe on the back of my head. Then everything plunged into darkness.

When I regained my senses, it was past midnight. The sky was clear as day. I did not know where I was for a moment. I saw the full moon hanging languidly for a moment. I opened my swollen eyes a little and the golden light of several stars appeared in the depth of the sky. Slowly I realized what had happened. And then, when I understood it all, tears rolled down my cheeks and fell on the cool carrot leaves underneath my head.

It was the final warning. When I reached our bunkhouse, my companions were crowded into the kitchen reading a roughly written message that had been thrown into the place that night. The men who had beaten me had driven to the bunkhouse when they were through with me.

One of the older men, who had known darker times in this land, took me by the arm and secreted me in the outer house, saying, "I could have told you these things before, but I saw that you were truly interested in educating yourself. I admired your courage and ambition. May I shake your hand?"

I said, taking his, "Thank you."

"Some men are good, but others are bad," he said. "But all evil is not confined in one race of people, nor all goodness in another. There is evil in every race, but there is also goodness in every other. And yet all the goodness belongs to the whole human race."

Then I knew why Miss O'Reilly had come to our bunkhouse and taught us. But I did not go to her boarding house for a week. I was afraid. When my bruises were well enough, I went to town, but Miss O'Reilly's room was closed and dark. I thought she had gone to a movie; I waited almost all night.

But she did not appear that night. Nor any other night. Then I knew that she had moved to another house, because during the day I saw her in the schoolyard. Sometimes she stopped and waved her hand toward us. I waved mine, too. And that went on for days. And then she disappeared.

I often wondered what had happened to her. Another teacher took her place. But the new teacher did not even notice us. So at night and on our days off we went to town in separate groups looking for our teacher. But we did not find her. We finished picking the peas and we transferred to the other side of the hill to harvest the tomatoes. Now and then we stopped to look toward the schoolhouse, but Miss O'Reilly did not come back. Then one day in June the schoolhouse closed its door and we watched the children slowly walk home. It was the end of another school year, but it was only the beginning of my first year in the new land.

One day, toward the end of the tomato season, Miss O'Reilly appeared. She looked a little thinner. I noticed a scar on her left wrist.

"I was in the hospital for a while," she greeted us. "I have been ill."

"You should have let us know," I said. "We would have sent you some flowers from the hill."

"That is nice of you," she said to me. "But now I am leaving. Going to the big city."

"Will you come back some day, Miss O'Reilly?" I asked.

"I hope so," she said. "But when you come to the big city, try to look for me. I think I'll be there for a long time."

"Are you going to teach in another school?"

"I don't know," she said. "But I will try to find an assignment. Yes, there must be a vacancy somewhere." And then, kindly, she put her hand on my head saying, "I will go on teaching people like you to understand things as long as the grass shall grow."

It was like a song. I did not know what she meant, but the words followed me down the years. That night we gave Miss O'Reilly a party at our bunkhouse. We roasted a pig in the open air. The men tuned up their musical instruments and played all night long. The moon was up in the sky and the sea was silent as ever. The tall mountains were still there; above them stars were shedding light to the world below. The grass on the hill was beginning to catch the morning dew. And then we took Miss O'Reilly to her car and bade her goodbye.

I wanted to cry. Tenderly she put her hand on my head.

"Remember," she said, "when you come to the city, try to look for me. And now, goodnight to all."

And she drove away. I never saw her again.

I went away from that town not long afterward and worked in many big cities. I would work for a long time in one place, but when the leaves of the trees started to fall, I would pack up my suitcase and go to another city. The years passed by very swiftly.

One morning I found I had been away from home for twenty years. But where is home? I saw the grass of another spring growing on the hills and in the fields. And the thought came to me that I had had Miss O'Reilly with me all the time, there in the broad fields and verdant hills of America, my home.

Life and Death of a Filipino in America

I first saw death when I was a small boy in the little village where I was born. It was a cool summer night and the sky was as clear as day and the ripening rice fields were golden in the moonlight. I remember that I was looking out the window and listening to the sweet mating calls of wild birds in the tall trees nearby when I heard my mother scream from the dark corner of the room where she had been lying for several days because she was big with child. I ran to her to see what was going on, but my grandmother darted from somewhere in the faint candlelight and held me close to the warm folds of her cotton skirt.

My mother was writhing and kicking frantically at the old woman who was attending her, but when the child was finally delivered and cleaned I saw that my mother was frothing at the mouth and slowly becoming still. She opened her eyes and tried to look for me in the semi-darkness, as though she had something important to tell me. Then she closed her eyes and lay very still.

My grandmother took me to the field at the back of our house and we sat silently under the bending stalks of rice for hours and once, when I looked up to push away the heavy grain that was tickling my neck, I saw the fleeting shadow of a small bird across the sky followed by a big bat. The small bird disappeared in the periphery of moonlight and darkness, shrieking fiercely when the bat caught up with it somewhere there beyond the range of my vision. Then I thought of my mother who had just died and my little brother who was born to take her place, but my thoughts of him created a terror inside me, and when my grandmother urged me to go back to the house, I burst into tears and clutched desperately at two huge stalks of rice so that she could not pull me away. My father came to the field then and carried me gently in his arms, and I clung tightly to him as though he alone could assuage my grief and protect me from all the world.

I could not understand why my mother had to die. I could not understand why my brother had to live. I was fearful of the motives of the living and the meaning of their presence on the earth. And I felt that my little brother, because he had brought upon my life a terrorizing grief, would be a stranger to me forever and ever. It was my first encounter with death; so great was its impress on my thinking that for years I could not forget my mother's pitiful cries as she lay dying.

My second encounter with death happened when I was ten years old. My father and I were plowing in the month of May. It was raining hard that day and our only working carabao was tired and balked at moving. This animal and I grew up together like brothers; he was my constant companion in the fields and on the hillsides at the edge of our village when the rice was growing.

My father, who was a kind and gentle man, started beating him with sudden fury. I remember that there was a frightening thunderclap somewhere in the world, and I looked up suddenly toward the eastern sky and saw a wide arc of vanishing rainbow. It was then that my father started beating our carabao mercilessly. The animal jumped from the mud and ran furiously across the field, leaving the wooden plow stuck into the trunk of a large dead tree. My father unsheathed his sharp bolo and raced after him, the thin blade of the steel weapon gleaming in the slanting rain. At the edge of a deep pit where we burned felled trees and huge roots, the carabao stopped and looked back; but sensing the anger of my father, he plunged headlong into the pit. I could not move for a moment, then I started running madly toward the pit.

My father climbed down the hole and looked at the carabao with tears in his eyes. I did not know if they were tears of madness or of repressed fury. But when I had climbed down after him, I saw big beads of sweat rolling down his forehead, mingling with his tears and soaking his already wet ragged farmer's clothes. The carabao had broken all his legs and he was trembling and twisting in the bottom of the pit. When my father raised the bolo in his hands to strike at the animal, I turned away and pressed my face in the soft embankment. Then I heard his hacking at the animal, grunting and cursing in the heavy rain.

When I looked again the animal's head was completely severed from the body, and warm blood was flowing from the trunk and making a red pool under our feet. I wanted to strike my father, but instead, fearing and loving him I climbed out of the pit quickly and ran through the blinding rain to our house.

Twice now I had witnessed violent deaths. I came across death again some years afterward on a boat when, on my way to America, I befriended a fellow passenger of my age named Marco.

He was an uneducated peasant boy from the northern part of our island who wanted to earn a little money in the new land and return to his village. It seemed there was a girl waiting for him when he came back, and although she was also poor and uneducated Marco found happiness in her small brown face and simple ways. He showed me a faded picture of her and ten dollars he had saved up to have it enlarged when we arrived in the new land.

Marco had a way of throwing back his head and laughing loudly, the way peasants do in that part of the island. But he was quick and sensitive; anger would suddenly appear in his dark face, then fear, and then laughter again; and sometimes all these emotions would simultaneously appear in his eyes, his mouth, his whole face. Yet he was sincere and honest in whatever he did or said to me.

I got seasick the moment we left Manila, and Marco started hiding oranges and apples in his suitcase for me. Fruits were the only things I could eat, so in the dead of the night when the other passengers were stirring in their bunks and peering through the dark to see what was going on, I sat up. Suddenly there was a scream and someone shouted for the light. I ran to the corner and clicked the switch and when the room was flooded with light, I saw Marco lying on the floor and bleeding from several knife wounds on his body. I knelt beside him, but for a moment only, because he held my hands tightly and died. I looked at the people around me and then asked them to help me carry the body to a more comfortable place. When the steward came down to make an inventory of Marco's suitcase, the ten dollars was gone. We shipped back the suitcase, but I kept the picture of the girl.

I arrived in America when thousands of people were waiting in line for a piece of bread. I kept on moving from town to town, from one filthy job to another, and then many years were gone. I even lost the girl's picture and for a while forgot Marco and my village.

I met Crispin in Seattle in the coldest winter of my life. He had just arrived in the city from somewhere in the east and he had no place to stay. I took him to my room and for days we slept together, eating what we could buy with the few cents that we begged in gambling houses from night to night. Crispin had drifted most of his life and he could tell me about other cities. He was very gentle and there was something luminous about him, like the strange light that flashes in my mind when I sometimes think of the hills of home. He had been educated and he recited poetry with a sad voice that made me cry. He always spoke of goodness and beauty in the world.

It was a new experience and the years of loneliness and fear were shadowed by the grace of his hands and the deep melancholy of his eyes. But the gambling houses were closed toward the end of that winter and we could not beg any more from the gamblers because they were also starving. Crispin and I used to walk in the snow for hours looking for nothing, waiting for the cold night to fall, hoping for the warm sun to come out of the dark sky. And then one night when we had not eaten for five days, I got out of bed and ate several pages of an old newspaper by soaking them in a can of water from the faucet in our room. Choking tears came out of my eyes, but the deep pain in my head burst wide open and blood came out of my nose. I finally went to sleep from utter exhaustion, but when I woke up again, Crispin was dead.

Yes, it was true. He was dead. He had not even contemplated death. Men like Crispin who had poetry in their souls come silently into the world and live quietly down the years, and yet when they are gone no moon in the sky is lucid enough to compare with the light they shed when they are among the living.

After nearly a decade of wandering and rootlessness, I lost another good friend who had guided me in times of helplessness. I was in California in a small agricultural community. I lived in a big bunkhouse of thirty farm workers with Leroy, who was a stranger to me in many ways because he was always talking about unions and unity. But he had a way of explaining the meanings of words in utter simplicity, like "work" which he translated into "power," and "power" into "security." I was drawn to him because I felt that he had lived in many places where the courage of men was tested with the cruelest weapons conceivable.

One evening I was eating with the others when several men came into our bunkhouse and grabbed Leroy from the table and dragged him outside. He had been just about to swallow a ball of rice when the men burst into the place and struck Leroy viciously on the neck with thick leather thongs. He fell on the floor and coughed up the ball of rice. Before Leroy realized what was happening to him, a big man came toward him from the darkness with a rope in his left hand and a shining shotgun in the other. He tied the rope around Leroy's neck while the other men pointed their guns at us, and when they had taken him outside, where he began screaming like a pig about to be butchered, two men stayed at the door with their aimed guns. There was some scuffling outside, then silence, and then the two men slowly withdrew with their guns, and there was a whispering sound of running feet on the newly cut grass in the yard and then the smooth purring of cars speeding away toward the highway and then there was silence again.

We rushed outside all at once, stumbling against each other. And there hanging on a tall eucalyptus tree, naked and shining in the pale light of the April moon, Leroy was swinging like a toy balloon. We cut him down and put him on the grass, but he died the moment we reached him. His genitals were cut and there was a deep knife wound in his chest. His left eye was gone and his tongue was sliced into tiny shreds. There was a wide gash across his belly and his entrails plopped out and spread on the cool grass.

That is how they killed Leroy. When I saw his cruelly tortured body, I thought of my father and the decapitated carabao and the warm blood flowing under our bare feet. And I knew that all my life I would remember Leroy and all the things he taught me about living.

Homecoming

Already, through the coming darkness, he could see landmarks of familiar places. He stirred as he looked out of the window, remembering scenes of childhood. Houses flew by him; the sudden hum of human activity reached his ears. He was nearing home.

He kept his eyes upon the narrowing landscape. When the bus drove into town and stopped under the big arbor tree that was the station, he rushed from his seat and jumped on to the ground, filled with joy and wonder and mystery.

The station was deserted. He found the old road that ran toward his father's house. He walked in the darkness, between two long rows of houses. A little dog shot out from a house and barked at him. He looked at it with a friendly smile. He wanted to stop and pick up a handful of the earth of home, but thoughts of his people loomed large in his mind. Every step brought vivid recollections of his family. He was bursting with excitement, not knowing what to say. He walked on in the thickening darkness.

He had gone to America 12 years before, when he was 15. And now that he was back, walking on the dirt road that he had known so well, he felt like a boy of 15 again.

Yes, he was barely 15 when he left home. He began to remember how one evening he ran like mad on this road with some roots that the herbalist needed for his mother, who was sick in bed with a mysterious disease. He had cried then, hugging the roots close to him. He knew that the fate of his mother was in his hands; he knew that they were waiting for him. . . . A mist came to his eyes. Reliving this tragic moment of childhood, he began to weaken with sudden tenderness for his mother. He walked faster, remembering. . . .

Then he came to the gate of his father's house. For some moments he stood before the house, his heart pounding painfully. And now he knew. This was what he had come for—a little grass house near the mountains, away from the riot and madness of cities. He had left the civilization of America for this tiny house, and now that he was here, alone, he felt weak inside. He was uncertain.

For a moment he was afraid of what the house would say; he was afraid of what the house would ask him. The journey homeward had been more than 8,000 miles of land and water, but now that he was actually standing before the house, it seemed as if he had come from a place only a few miles away.

He surveyed the house in the dark, lost in his memories. Then he stepped forward, his feet whispering in the sand that filled the path to the house.

A faint gleam of light from the kitchen struck his face. He recalled at once that when he was young, the family always came home late in the evening; and his mother, who did all the domestic chores, served dinner around midnight. He paused a while, feeling a deep love for his mother. Then he crawled under the window, where the light shot across his face. He stood there and waited, breathless, for a moment.

But they were very quiet in the house. He could hear somebody moving toward the stove and stopping there to pour water into a jar. He found a hard object which he knew to be an empty box, and he hoisted himself on it, looking into the kitchen whence the lamp threw a beam of soft light.

Now he could see a large portion of the kitchen. He raised his heels, his eyes roving over the kitchen. Then he caught a quick glimpse of his mother, the old oil lamp in her hand. He was petrified with fear, not knowing what to do. One foot slipped from the side of the box and he hung in mid-air. He wanted to shout to her all the sorrows of his life, but a choking lump came to his throat. He looked, poised, and undecided; then his mother disappeared behind a yellow curtain. His mind was a riot of conflict; he shifted from foot to foot. But action came to him at last. He jumped on to the ground and ran to the house.

He climbed up the ladder and stood by the door. His younger sister was setting the table, and his older sister, who was called Francisca, was helping his mother with the boiling pot on the stove. He watched the three women moving mechanically in the kitchen. Then he stepped forward, his leather shoes slapping against the floor. Francisca turned toward him and screamed.

"Mother!"

The mother looked swiftly from the burning stove and found the bewildered face of her son.

"It's me—Mariano—" He moved toward them, pausing at the table. "Mother!"

They rushed to him, all of them; the moment was eternity. Marcela, the younger sister, knelt before him; she was crying wordlessly. The mother was in his arms; her white hair fell upon his shoulder. Unable to say anything sensible, he reached for Francisca and said: "You've grown. . . ."

Francisca could not say a word; she turned away and wept. The tension of this sudden meeting was unbearable to him. And now he was sorry he had come home. He felt that he could never make them happy again; a long period of deterioration would follow this sudden first meeting. He knew it, and he revolted against it. But he also knew that he could never tell them why he had come home.

They prepared a plate for him. He was hungry and he tried to eat everything they put on his plate. They had stopped eating. They were waiting for him to say something; they were watching his every movement. There were many things to talk about, but he did not know where to begin. He was confused. The silence was so deep he could hear the wind among the trees outside. Pausing a while, a thought came to his mind. *Father:* Where was father? Where could father be?

He looked at Francisca. "Where is Father?" he asked.

Francisca turned to her mother for guidance, then at Mariano's lifted face.

Finally, Francisca said: "Father died a year after you left."

"Father was a very old man," Marcela added. "He died in his sleep."

Mariano wanted to believe them, but he felt that they were only trying to make it easy for him. Then he looked at his mother. For the first time he seemed to realize that she had aged enormously. Then he turned to his sisters, who had become full-grown women in his absence. A long time passed before he could say anything.

"I didn't know that," he said, looking down at his food.

"We didn't want you to know," his mother said.

"I didn't know that father died," he repeated.

"Now you know," Marcela said.

Mariano tried to swallow the hot rice in his mouth, but a big lump of pain came to his throat. He could not eat any more. He washed his hands and reached for the cloth on the wall above the table.

"I've had enough," he said.

Marcela and Francisca washed the dishes in a tall wooden tub. The mother went to the living room and spread the thin mat on the floor. Mariano sat on the long bench, near the stove. He was waiting for them to ask questions. His eyes roved around the house, becoming intimate with the furniture. When the mother came to the kitchen, Marcela took the lamp from the wall and placed it on one end of the bench. The light rose directly toward Mariano's face.

The mother paused. "Why didn't you let us know you were coming?" she asked.

"I wanted to surprise you," he lied.

"I'm glad you are with us again."

"We're very glad," Francisca said.

"Yes," Marcela said.

Then the mother closed the window. Mariano looked at Marcela, but the light dazzled him. Now he felt angry with himself. He wanted to tell the truth, but could not. How could he make them understand that he had failed in America? How could he let them realize that he had come home because there was no other place for him in the world? At 27, he felt through with life; he knew that he had come home to die. America had crushed his spirit.

He wanted to say something, but did not know were to begin. He was confused, now that he was home. All he could say was: "I came home . . ."

A strong wind blew into the house, extinguishing the lamp. The house was thrown into complete darkness. He could hear Marcela moving around, fumbling for matches under the stove. In the brief instant of darkness that wrapped the house he remembered his years in the hospital. He recalled the day of his operation, when the doctor had worked on his right lung. It all came back to him. Strange: unconsciously, he placed a hand on his chest. When the match spurted in Marcela's cupped palms, Mariano drew away his hand. He watched the lamp grow brighter until the house was all lighted again.

Then he said: "I wanted to write, but there was nothing I could say."

"We knew that," the mother said.

They were silent. Mariano looked at their faces. He knew now that he could never tell them what the doctor had told him before he sailed for home. Two years perhaps, the doctor had said. Yes, he had only two years left to live in the world. Two years: How much could he do in so brief a time? He began to feel weak. He looked at their faces.

Now it was his turn. Touching Marcela by the hand, he asked: "Are you all right? I mean . . . since father died . . ."

"I take laundry from students," Marcela said. "But it's barely enough. And sister here—"

Francisca rose suddenly and ran to the living room. The mother looked at Marcela. The house was electrified with fear and sadness.

"When students go back to their hometowns, we have nothing."

"Is Francisca working?"

"She takes care of the Judge's children. Sister doesn't like to work in that house, but it's the only available work in town."

His heart was dying slowly.

"Mother can't go around any more. Sister and I work to the bones. We've never known peace."

Mariano closed his eyes for a brief moment and pushed the existence of his sister out of his consciousness. The mother got up from the floor and joined Francisca in the living room. Now Mariano could hear Francisca weeping. Marcela was tougher; she looked toward the living room with hard, unsentimental eyes. Mariano was frightened, knowing what Marcela could do in a harsh world.

"Sister isn't pretty any more," Marcela said.

Mariano was paralyzed with the sudden fear. He looked at Marcela. *Yes, she too was not pretty any more.* But she did not care about herself; she was concerned over her sister. He looked at her cotton dress, torn at the bottom. Then he felt like smashing the whole world; he was burning with anger. He was angry against all the forces that had made his sisters ugly.

Suddenly, he knelt before Marcela. He took her hands, comprehending. Marcela's palms were rough. Her finger-nails were torn like matchsticks. Mariano bit his lower lip until it bled. He knew he would say something horrible if he opened his mouth. Instead he got up and took the lamp and went to the living room.

Francisca was weeping in her mother's arms. Mariano held the lamp above them, watching Francisca's face. She turned her face away, ashamed. But Mariano saw, and now he knew. *Francisca was not pretty any more.* He wanted to cry.

"We were hungry," Marcela said. She had followed him.

Mariano turned around suddenly and felt cold inside when he saw Marcela's cold stare in the semi-darkness. What did he not know about hunger? *Goddamn!*

"I wish I . . ." he stopped. Fear and anger welled up in him. Now he could understand the brevity of his answers to his questions; their swift glances that meant more than their tongues could utter. Now he could understand his mother's deadening solemnity. And Marcela's bitterness. Now it dawned on him that his mother and sisters had suffered the same terrors of poverty, the same humiliations of defeat, that he had suffered in America. He was like a man who had emerged from night into day, and found the light as blinding as the darkness.

The mother knelt on the floor, reaching for the lamp. Mariano walked back to the kitchen. He knew he could not do anything for them. He knew he could not do anything for himself. He knew he could not do anything at all. This was the life he had found in America; it was so everywhere in the world. He thought when he was in America that it could not be thus in his father's house. But it was there when he returned to find his sisters wrecked by deprivation . . .

Mariano stood by the window long after they had gone to bed. He stood in the darkness, waiting. The houses were silent. The entire district was quiet as a tomb. His mother was sleeping peacefully. He turned to look at his sisters in the dark. They were sleeping soundly. Then noiselessly, he walked to the bed.

Mariano leaned against the wall, thinking. After a while a child began to cry somewhere in the neighborhood. Two dogs ran across the road, chasing each other. Then a rooster began to crow and others followed. It was almost dawn.

Now Mariano sat still in the darkness, listening. When he was sure they were deep in sleep, he got up slowly and reached for his hat on the table. He stopped at the door and looked back. He found a match in his pocket and scratched it on the panel of the door. Then he tiptoed to his mother and watched her face with tenderness. As he walked over to his sisters, the match burned out. He stood between them, trembling with indecision. Suddenly, he walked to the door and descended the ladder in a hurry.

There were a few stars in the sky. The night wind was soft. There was a touch of summer in the air. When he had passed the gate, Mariano stopped and looked back at the house. The vision of his father rose in the night. Then it seemed to him that the house of his childhood was more vivid than at any other time in that last look. He knew he would never see it again.

The Thief

His name was Cesar Terso. Nobody knew him twenty years ago. Some say that he borrowed his name from an unknown Philippine poet. Others say it was his real name. I saw him in Salinas in the summer of 1933. He had been in this country eight years then, and his exploits were beginning to assume the fantastic proportions that spread among our people.

It was the leanest year of my life. I had been traveling through California, sometimes on foot, sometimes in the freight trains. Once I tried to cross the country, went as far as Montana where the cold winter stopped me. I returned to California through Nevada, passing through the tunnels between that state and California. I went to Stockton and tried to find some work at the packing houses there. Then I proceeded to San Jose, and from there I went to Salinas.

The cold winter was almost over. Salinas, however, was still teeming with migratory farm workers. For days I walked on Soledad Street and sat in the Chinese gambling houses.

It was in a little Mexican restaurant where I met Cesar Terso. I remember the hour vividly because a few years afterward all of us who were there remembered him.

He was drinking in a booth with three young men. They probably belonged to the same tribe in the Philippines because there was something similar in their faces. He was the youngest in the group. Suddenly one of the fellows with him, who had been forced to stop his studies at the University of Washington due to financial reasons, said aloud: "I need a few hundreds of that filthy money in the Chinese gambling house!"

Cesar said quietly, "Will you go back to the University if I give you some money?"

His companions thought he was joking. The student found some money in his drawer one morning, so he went back to the University of

Washington. Upon graduation he returned to Manila and taught ichthyology at the University of the Philippines. Later he was awarded a Guggenheim Fellowship for having discovered a new way to hatch salmon eggs.

Cesar Terso's career started that night in Salinas. He traveled up and down the coast, helping destitute Filipino students. Once I heard that he robbed a gambling house in Seattle, and five Chinese were killed in the commotion. He had nothing to do with the murders. Throughout his career he never hurt anybody.

The Seattle affair spread throughout the Pacific Coast. It was at that time that Chinese and Japanese vice-lords started hiring Filipino killers to protect their business. Then a gambling house was burned in Stockton, and suddenly a destitute Mexican-Filipino family became luxurious. It was rumored that Cesar Terso had something to do with these mysterious bounties.

What fascinated me was his kindness toward poor students. I think he had sent to school more than a dozen Filipinos, and five of them made names for themselves in the Philippines.

I saw Cesar Terso again in 1948. I was then living in Los Angeles. It was sixteen years after I first saw him. He had become a different person. He had just arrived from Chicago and he did not know where to go next. One evening I invited him to my room where we sat and talked. Then we went out and walked in the streets.

It was New Year's Eve. He started to tell me about his life, and for the first time I began to understand him. I tried to piece the fragments together, and suddenly I discovered that I was also piecing the fragments of my life together. I was then beginning to write, and I felt like writing the complete story of his life.

Cesar Terso was a genius, but adverse conditions distorted his mind. What could have been a positive contribution to society became a destructive weapon.

Cesar Terso disappeared again that year. I did not hear from him again for quite some time. He wrote me from Oklahoma where, he said, he had found the girl of his dreams. I knew marriage was not in his cards. Some weeks later I received a card from him. He was in San Francisco, where he was waiting for a "big stake." The big day came, but he was caught. Poor man, poor Cesar Terso!

But another decade of Filipino life in the U.S. had been ushered in. Cesar's generation had grown old and weary. Cesar Terso was tried and deported to the Philippines. I received a letter from him a few weeks ago. He did not mention anything about his activities. But I knew that he would rob somebody to send a poor boy to school.

It is because of my association with Cesar Terso that I write this brief story about him. Yes, there is a Robin Hood for every oppressed people. Legend sometimes becomes a weapon when a people that is oppressed too long remembers heroes like Cesar Terso. I know that another such character will be born out of the chaos of Filipino life in this country. But he will be a different hero, intelligent, political, human, and charged with a wonderful dream of a better America. . . .

The End of the War

It was a fine Sunday morning and the First Filipino Infantry was very quiet. Private Pascual Fidel, who was small even for a Filipino, opened his eyes and kicked the thick Army blankets off his body. His right hand reached for the shiny harmonica which was on the floor beside a pair of clean boots. He rubbed his eyes slowly and then began humming, "Amor, amor, amor," which he had heard on the radio some nights before. He tapped the harmonica on his knee, out of habit, put it in his mouth, and fumbled for the first note. Suddenly his hands stopped and he jumped up and ran around the room from cot to cot, looking. But his comrades had already left. With nothing on but his undershorts, he rushed through the door of the barracks and out into the bright sunlight, screaming for his cousin, "Pitong! Sergeant Pitong Tongkol!"

Sergeant Tongkol, who was in the same company of the First Filipino Infantry, stood watching three men planting poppies in a vacant space nearby. He looked up and saw Private Fidel running toward him. Anxious to know what it was all about, Sergeant Tongkol started to meet his cousin. They met in front of the mess hall, where most of the soldiers were now assembled.

"What is it, Cousin?" Sergeant Tongkol asked.

"I had a dream," Private Fidel said, when he had caught his breath.

"A dream?" Sergeant Tongkol said.

"It is a big dream," Private Fidel said. "It is bigger than this whole camp." He stopped and looked beyond Sergeant Tongkol at the distant low brown hills of northern California. Then, turning around slowly, he scanned the vastness of the valley that surrounded Camp Beale.

"What happened, Cousin?" Sergeant Tongkol asked.

"We were approaching Mindanao when it happened," Private Fidel said. "I remember it very well because I was playing monte with my brother Malong and your brother Ponso when it happened. I had a poor hand, so I wanted to cheat, because it was my last dollar." He spread an imaginary hand of cards in front of his cousin, and while Sergeant Tongkol became more and more impatient, Private Fidel deliberated as if he were actually playing cards. Finally he said, "Your brother Ponso put two dollars in the pot, but my brother Malong raised the bet. I had a pair of threes, but there was another three under my left foot. I remember it well because my eyes were not on my cards; they were glued to the approaching shore of southern Mindanao. I saw Ponso's helmet move in the morning light when I reached for the hidden card. Then it happened, suddenly and without ceremony."

"What happened?" Sergeant Tongkol asked.

"I ran to the railing of the ship and looked," Private Fidel continued. "I stood there for quite some time, not believing in what I saw. But it was true. They came to the shore and surrendered."

"What is true?" Sergeant Tongkol shouted. "Who surrendered? As your superior, Private Fidel, I order you to answer me!" He stepped back and stood at attention, waiting for his cousin to obey him.

"The Japs met us on the beach and surrendered," Private Fidel said. "A few minutes afterward, it was broadcast that Germany had also surrendered and the war came to a sudden end."

Sergeant Tongkol was stunned for a moment. Then, realizing the importance of the event, he grabbed his cousin and a rush of anxious words poured out of his mouth. "Are you sure, Cousin?" he asked. "Are you sure they were Japs? Did you see the large teeth of the yellow sons of the Rising Sun? Did you hear the broadcast that the war came to an end?"

"I'm sure, Sergeant Tongkol!" Private Fidel shouted.

Sergeant Tongkol relaxed his hold. His face was filled with sudden kindness. "Not so loud, Cousin," he said. "Here is my jacket. You might catch cold."

Private Fidel put the jacket on. It was so big that it hung like an overcoat. Filled now with the big dream, Sergeant Tongkol expanded his chest. Wild anticipation illumined his eyes and his dark face. He put his arm around Private Fidel, as though his cousin were a precious toy. "Let's tell the good news to my brother," Sergeant Tongkol said.

The two Filipino soldiers walked eagerly toward the mess hall, each with his arm around the other. It was always like that with Private Fidel and Sergeant Tongkol. They were the same age and in their native village, on the island of Luzon, they used to go together into the banana grove across the river and steal the choicest fruit. They sailed together to the United States when they were seventeen years old. They had worked together on a farm most of the time since, and they were never separated from each other except when one of them was in jail for gambling or selling something that did not belong to him. When the war came, they had volunteered together. But it had been hard on Private Fidel when, some months after their enlistment, his cousin Pitong was promoted. Pitong had always been his inferior in civilian life, especially when they were working on the farm. Sergeant Tongkol had been just a field hand, cutting lettuce or picking tomatoes or doing some unimportant job like that. But he, Private Fidel, was a bookkeeper or timekeeper or had some other important job. He resented his cousin's promotion and he had tried many times to work against him, but every time was discredited. He had resigned himself to his fate and did not even try for promotions except in his dreams, where one promotion after another came to him.

Mess Sergeant Ponso Tongkol was chopping string beans into a barrel with a long butcher knife. When the two soldiers approached him, he started chopping faster. His feet danced rhythmically as he jabbed the knife up and down. It was a stunt they always enjoyed. The two soldiers stood watching him. Suddenly Sergeant Pitong grabbed his brother. "The war has ended, Ponso!" he said.

One of the dancing feet stopped in mid-air. The butcher knife stopped moving up and down. Slowly, Ponso looked up from the barrel of chopped string beans and his eyes fastened on his brother's face. "You are kidding, Brother," he said. "But it is true, Ponso," Sergeant Pitong said.

Mess Sergeant Ponso sat down on the edge of the barrel and put the knife in his lap. "If it is true that the war has ended," he said, "why am I still preparing string beans for dinner?"

"It is in the dream that the war had ended," Private Fidel interrupted.

Sergeant Pitong pushed him away and planted himself in front of his brother. "We were approaching Mindanao when it happened," he began, glancing sideways at Private Fidel with his superior air. "I remember it vividly, because I was walking on the deck with his brother Malong."

"No, no!" Private Fidel protested. "I was there!"

"Let me tell it," Sergeant Pitong said. "This dream is not for a small potato like you, Private Fidel." Then he turned his back on him and faced the mess sergeant. "I was walking on the deck with Private Fidel's brother Malong when it happened. I was about to tell him about a champion gamecock I had when I was in Salinas, California. That rooster had the most beautiful pair of legs. I made lots of money betting on him, but it was not the money that I enjoyed as much as his dancing feet when he was in the ring with an adversary. Well, then, it was at this moment when it happened. The Japs came to the shore and surrendered. Then it was broadcast that the war had ended."

"Was the Son of Heaven with the soldiers?" Mess Sergeant Ponso asked.

"He was the first one to come to the shore," Sergeant Pitong said.

Private Fidel interrupted again. "He was *not* there. The Emperor was not there. I would have seen him and his white horse if they'd been there."

"He *was* there!" Sergeant Pitong said. "The Son of Heaven came to meet us with several generals. They were all smiling and willing to surrender."

"The salomabit!"* Mess Sergeant Ponso exclaimed. He gripped the handle of the butcher knife with both hands. "Then what did you do?"

"We started shouting and throwing away our guns," his brother said.

"Goddamit!" Mess Sergeant Ponso shouted, getting up from the barrel. Slowly he sat down again. "If I was only there," he said. The strong hands tightened around the knife. He was a much larger man than his brother. He got up once more and walked around a table, stabbing the air furiously with the knife.

"It was only a dream," Private Fidel said.

But Mess Sergeant Ponso did not hear him. He said, "Ten years I

---

*"Son of a bitch" in the Filipino idiom.

worked peacefully in America, minding my own business, when the salomabit come stabbing me at the back. Maybe it is not much I make, but I got the beautiful Ford from Detroit. When I come home at night from work, I ride it to town, pressing the horn and whistling. I ride and ride and I am happy. In the bank I got money—maybe not much, but it is my money. When I see the flag, I take the hat off and I say, "Thank you very much!" I like the color of the flag and I work hard. Why the *salomabit* come?" He drove the knife into the edge of the table with a terrific blow. Then he looked at his brother and cousin. "If only I was there!"

Private Fidel stepped back. He was not afraid of his cousin, but he kept his eyes on the knife nevertheless. Mess Sergeant Ponso pulled the knife out and wiped it with his apron. Then he produced a bottle of wine from the rice bin and filled three glasses. As though he had noticed Private Fidel for the first time, Mess Sergeant Ponso pulled a pair of pants from a hook on the wall and gave it to him. "Here," he said, "put these on. And then let's tell the good news to your brother."

The three soldiers hurried from the mess hall and went to the latrine, where Private Malong Fidel was on duty. When he saw them rushing toward him, he dropped the handle of his mop.

"The war has come to an end, Malong," Mess Sergeant Ponso said.

Private Malong stepped back against the wall of the latrine. . . . "Don't torture me," he said. "I'm too tired."

"But it's true!" Mess Sergeant Ponso shouted. "I saw the Son of Heaven himself, and his wife—"

Sergeant Pitong tried to interrupt, but his brother prevented him by putting a huge hand over his mouth.

"No, no!" Private Fidel cried. "I was there!" The loud voice of his cousin Ponso drowned him out.

Private Fidel had dreamed the big dream, but it was too big for him to hold. It was a dream that belonged to no one now, yet it was a dream for every soldier. Hearing it told by another person, Private Fidel knew that it was not his dream anymore. First it had become Sergeant Pitong's dream, then Mess Sergeant Ponso had taken it over. In a few minutes, it would be Malong's dream.

In utter defeat, Private Fidel backed out into the sunlight and returned to his barracks where he sat on his cot. He was surprised to notice that the harmonica was still in his hand. He tapped it on his knee, out of habit, and started to play, "Amor, Amor, Amor." After a while, he began playing with great joy and inspiration.

Essays

How My Stories Were Written

A few years ago, I wrote for the *Writer* a brief article revealing the compelling force that propelled me from an obscure occupation to the rewarding writing of short stories. That *force* was anger born of a rebellious dissatisfaction with everything around me.

When I sold my first story, I was still a laborer at a fish cannery in San Pedro, California. But immediately afterward letters came asking me how I became a writer, pointedly emphasizing the fact that I have a very limited formal education, and why was I writing proficiently in a language which is not my own?

The making of a writer is not by accident. It takes years of painstaking preparation, whether one knows or not that he is on the path of a writing career; of extensive reading of significant contemporary writings and the classics of literature, and of intensive experimental writing, before one is ready to synthesize reading, writing and experience into a solid premise from which one should begin a difficult career as a writer.

But the type of writing which flows from such a premise depends completely on the sensibility of the individual and his ability to crystallize his thoughts; whether he would interpret reality and maintain that art is not alien to life but a transmutation of it in artistic terms, or indifferently deny life and completely escape from it, as though the immediacy of man's problems of existence were not the concern of the writer.

I did not know what kind of a writer I would become. Not having known any writer personally, I had to grope my way in the dark. And what a heartbreaking journey that was! I thought I could write commercial stories for the high-paying slick magazines—and thus I wrote dozens of stories that came back as fast as I sent them out. Then the foolish notion came to me that the literary magazines were my natural field, since the literary story seemed to me the easiest thing to write; so dozens of stories again came back as fast as I sent them out.

Remember that these stories dealt with a life that was unknown to me. I wrote about imagined experiences of body and mind, put words in the mouths of characters that were ridiculously alien to them, it seems to me now. I even carefully plotted: the compulsive beginning, the staggering anti-climax or denouement, and the heartwarming or heart-breaking climax.

You see, I denied myself: my own experiences seemed irrelevant, my own thoughts seemed innocuous, my own perceptions seemed chaotic and ambiguous. These are some of the dilemmas of the beginner.

It was only when I began to write about the life and people I have known that a certain measure of confidence began to form as my periscope for future writing. And as this confidence grew and took a definite shape, I discovered that the actual process of writing was easy—almost as easy as breathing.

I wrote about my family and the village where I had been born. I wrote about my friends and myself in America, placing my characters in localities familiar to me, and always wrapping them up in contemporary events. Except, of course, my stories based on Philippine folk tales and legends. But even these were given a background known to me. And more, I humanized my legendary and folktale characters, so that reading them, it would be impossible to determine which is fact and which is the flight of imagination.

I have written many stories of this type. I will now tell you about the vast storehouse of rich material with which my childhood world endowed me so generously that I can go on indefinitely writing folkwise stories based on the hard core of reality. It is about an old man in my childhood.

It is true there are mountains which are green all the year round bordering the northside of the province of Pangasinan, my own native province, in the island of Luzon. It is true there is a fertile valley under the shadows of these mountains from which the peasants have been scratching a living since the dawn of Philippine history. And these simple peasants, backward still in their ways and understanding of the world, have not yet discarded the primitive tools that their forefathers had used centuries before them, in the beginning of a settlement that was to become the most densely packed population section of the island. The passing of time and the intensification of settlers in this valley helped preserve a common folklore that was related from mouth to mouth and from generation to generation, until it was no longer possible to distinguish which tale was indigenous to the people living there and which one was borrowed from the other tribes and molded into their own. But the telling of these tales was so enchanting, so uncommonly charming, that no man now questions the truth of their origin and the validity of their existence in times past.

It is also true that there is a village called Namgusmana, where I had been born, in this valley where a wayward river runs uncharted and waters the plains on its journey to the open seas. Here the farmers plant rice when the rains come from the mountains to the north, and corn when the sun shines, and sugarcane when soothing winds blow from the other horizon in the south and sometimes in the west, so that the fields are verdant with vegetation every day of the year.

But it is also true that when the moon was bright in the sky an old man whose age no one could remember because he was born long, long ago, in the era of the great distress of the land, who came down from his mysterious dwelling in the mountains and walked in our village and the children stoned him when he did not tell his tales of long ago: now it is true that he sometimes sat under a mango tree at the edge of the village to relate a story over a cup of red wine or when he was given a handful of boiled rice, and the children would scatter attentively on the grass around him, and the men and women would stand silently further away to catch every word, because there was no telling when he had a new tale about the people who had wandered and lived and died in that valley ages ago.

It happens that it is also true, that I heard this old man tell his tales many a time when I was a little boy. At first he did not notice my presence among the crowd of children that listened to him, but as time went by he began to notice me until at last he concentrated his telling to me.

"I have noticed your attentiveness," he said to me one day. "Do you believe these tales?"

"I believe them, Apo Lacay," I told him.

"But why?" he demanded. "These are merely the tales of an old and forgotten man who has lived beyond his time. There are others who can tell you more fascinating stories of what is happening today."

"There is wisdom in your words, Apo Lacay," I said respectfully. "Besides, I will go away some day and I would like to remember what kind of people lived here a long time past."

"You will go to a land far away," he asked. There was a sudden gleam in his eyes but just as suddenly it vanished, and a deep melancholy spread across his wrinkled face. "But you will never return, never come back to this valley."

I could not answer him then, or the day after, or long afterward—not even when I came to this land far away, remembering him.

"Everybody dies, but no man comes home again," he said sadly. "No man comes to bathe in the cool water of the river, to watch the golden grain in the fields, to know the grandeur of the meadow lark on the wing. No man comes back to feel the green loam of the land with his bare feet, to touch the rich soil with his loving hands, to see the earth move under him as he walks under his silent skies."

"I will come back, Apo Lacay," I said.

He looked at me silently and long, then there were tiny tears in his eyes.

"Son," he said at last, touching my head with his faded hands, "I will go home now."

He reached for his cane and walked away. He did not come again. Many years passed, and everybody thought he was dead. And then that year of my grand awakening, I decided to look for the old man. I went to the mountains and looked for him, sleeping in several forests and crossing many ravines and hills, shouting in the wind and climbing the tallest trees to see some signs of human habitation on the caves that dotted the mountainside. And at last I found him sitting by a small stream.

"Good morning, Apo Lacay," I greeted him.

He stirred but his face was lifted toward the sun.

"I came to say goodbye," I told him.

"So it is you,"he said. "I thought you left long ago."

"Now is the time, Apo Lacay," I said. "But tell me this: is it not dangerous to live all by yourself in the mountains?"

"What is there to fear in the night? The beasts, the birds, the trees, the storms and tempests—would you be afraid of them? There is nothing to fear in the night, in the heart of night. But in the daylight among men, there is the greatest fear."

"Buy why, Apo Lacay?"

"In the savage heart of man there dwells the greatest fear among the living."

"But man has a mind."

"That is the seed of all the fear. The mind of man. The beast in the jungle with his ferocious fangs is less dangerous than man with his cultivated mind. It is the heart that counts. The heart is everything, son."

"Is that why you tell the kind of stories you have told us? To make us laugh?"

"Laughter is the beginning of wisdom."

"There is perhaps a great truth in what you have just said. That is why I came to see you. I will leave our country soon and I would like to remember all your stories."

"But why? In that land where you are going, will the people give you something to eat when you retell them? Will you not be afraid the children will stone you?"

"I don't know, Apo Lacay. But this I know: if the retelling of your stories will give me a little wisdom of the heart, then I shall have come home again."

"You mean it will be your book as well as mine? Your words as well as my words, there in that faraway land, my tales going around to the people? My tales will not be forgotten at last?"

"Yes, Apo Lacay. It will be exactly like that, your books as well as mine."

He was silent for a long time. He made a fire by the stream, sat by it and contemplated deeply. Then it seemed to me, watching him lost in thought, he had become a little boy again living all the tales he had told us about a vanished race, listening to the gorgeous laughter of men in the midst of abject poverty and tyranny. For that was the time of his childhood, in the age of great distress and calamity in the land, when the fury of an invading race impaled their hearts in the tragic cross of slavery and ignorance. And that was why they had all become that way, sick in soul and mind, devoid of humanity, living like beasts in the jungle of their captivity. But this man who had survived them all, surviving a full century of change and now living in the first murmurs of a twilight and the dawn of reason and progress, was the sole surviving witness of the cruelty and dehumanization of man by another man, but whose tales were taken for laughter and the foolish words of a lonely old man who had lived far beyond his time.

When I looked at him again he was already dead. His passing was so quiet and natural that I did not feel any sadness. I dug a grave by the stream and buried him with the soft murmur of the trees all around me. Then I walked down the mountains and into the valley of home, but which was no longer a home. Sometime afterward I boarded a big boat that took me to this land far away.

And now in America, writing many years later, I do not exactly know which were the words of the old man of the mountains and which are mine. But they are his tales as well as mine, so I hope we have written stories that really belong to everyone in that valley beautiful beyond any telling of it.

The Growth of Philippine Culture

The growth of Philippine culture is closely linked with its political and economic history. It was a long-drawn and encumbered movement, but it was also a continuous and courageous struggle toward reality. Before monarchist Spain acquired the Philippines by discovery in 1521, under the leadership of Ferdinand Magellan who sacrificed his life for it, a considerable culture was developed. This culture took nourishments from the prodigal cultures brought by adventurous traders and missionaries from neighboring islands and countries. It was revealed in competence and excellence five hundred years later, when Spanish domination was broken by the most eloquent writers and thinkers who sponsored the upsurge of native cultural revival.

Politically, pre-Spanish Philippines was more advanced than the city-states of Europe during the same period due to its social structure which was based on a communal economy. It was this energizing economic arrangement which gave impetus to the birth and growth of a native culture that reached its highest development in the Shri-Visayan and Madjapahit empires. The flowering of this civilization which flourished throughout Asia and the Philippines was Buddhistic in character. Today there are still considerable remnants of this civilization in the southern part of the Philippine archipelago where Mohammedanism took a deep root in the life and thinking of the people.

Some of the first Spanish colonizers were dreamers and idealists who were principally concerned with the spreading of the positive virtues of Christianity in the islands. They were mostly members of the ecclesiastical orders. They were truly self-sacrificing and magnanimous to the natives, even to the point of paternalism. But the discovery of a new economic empire gave birth also to the rise of a gregarious power within the ecclesiastical hierarchy of Spain. Consequently the first colonizers were removed and gave way to the invasion of the new religious hierarchy that brought with it greed, superimposed by an accompanying political tyranny. These worked together in the merciless exploitation of the newly discovered natural wealth and manpower in the islands until the religious orders, because they had a firmer hold on the imagination of the natives, became the dominant authority in Spain's colonial policy. As a consequence, when Spanish authority became utterly abusive and destructive, it paved the way to its shameful defeat and complete annihilation.

But the intellectual stupor that permeated the life of the people lasted a long time, so long that toward the end of the seventeenth century they nearly lost their cultural heritage. The church was the imperious vehicle of destruction and oppression; it instituted repressive measures against the continuation of an historical tradition which was at one time vigorous and promising. It violently uprooted every independent native cultural growth, imposing ignorance and illiteracy upon the people. Significantly, however, it was during this period of intellectual darkness that Francisco Balagtas, the first Filipino writer of historical importance, wrote *Florante at Laura*, which was the first notable creative work that attacked Spanish tyranny.

Spain was able to subjugate the Philippines for nearly four centuries of terror and cultural annihilation. But this condition could not exist forever in a land that had once known freedom, and among a people in whose conscience the dignity of man had been revealed. The exploitation of the islands uncovered a tremendous natural wealth, and this eventually led to the exposure of the Philippines. It was also the beginning of the rapid development of its economy; and this was the historical factor that led to the culmination of Spanish domination over the islands, leaving only those aspects of European civilization which were conducive to native cultural growth. The exposure of the Philippines to widescale trade and commerce was also the beginning of a positive cultural contact with the civilized world. It signalized the birth of a political awakening that grew and spread throughout the archipelago until the Filipinos rediscovered the strength and magnificence of their cultural heritage.

While the Filipinos were divided by the later colonizers, this awakening was an intellectual force that led them to discover a common social denominator on which they would work together toward the liberation of their country from foreign oppression. Even rudimentary education was still denied them; participation in the government was opened only to Spaniards and in limited degree to some affluent native families who bribed their way to secondary positions. Naturally, this confluence of native wealth and influence was the decisive factor that drove away the masses from the government and their own leaders since they represented only their interests and the policies of Spain.

However, not all wealthy Filipinos played this shameful role. A few far-sighted families saw the impossibility of a continued subjugation of the Philippines under these conditions; and they started the agitation, not for complete severance from the mother country, but for liberal reforms, active participation in the government, and representation in the Spanish Cortes. Taxation without representation had a dynamic effect on the natives, especially on those who were following the course of the French Revolution and the progress of the young American Republic; liberal reforms, participation, and representation were the three overall programs which the enlightened leaders concretized into a common action of unity, and from this the stage was set for mass agitation and propaganda until the people wrested it away from them.

Before this anti-climax was reached, the Filipino families of means, realizing that education in the Philippines was restricted but that they were unable to liberate and universalize it for lack of a united political action, went to the most advanced cities in Europe. This was at the beginning of the nineteenth century when nearly all European countries were in turmoil and the peoples were revolting against monarchy. These Filipinos saw the crumbling citadels of kings and other royalties; they often returned to the Philippines inspired by and inflamed with the fiery cultural movements abroad. They witnessed the political maelstrom that was reshaping the social structures of many countries in Europe, and from this they found an educational pattern for the enlightenment of their countrymen. More specially, the valiant example of the short-lived Spanish Republic awakened them to the grave wrongs that their people were suffering at home.

With the cooperation of republican Spaniards they formed a program of united political action in Madrid, which spread to Paris, Heidelberg, and London, and finally to Hongkong and Manila, and then to the rest of the Philippines where a coordinated struggle was effected with native leaders. There appeared a body of revolutionary literature which had its fountainhead in the Filipino colony in Madrid, and that moved on to Paris when Spain was again under the iron heel of the monarchy. Wherever there were Filipino colonies, this new literature spread in the capitals of Europe simultaneously with the growing underground movement in the Philippines, a mass movement that was to decide which of the social classes was best prepared and suited to handle the problems of independence and the construction of freedom's edifice.

Out of this period came a stream of writing truly political in nature. Its most ardent exponents were M. H. del Pilar, Graciano Lopez-Jaena, and Jose Rizal. The first two were propagandists who had escaped persecution and perhaps the Spanish garrote in the Philippines; in Madrid they edited *La Solidaridad,* a newspaper designed to arouse the sympathies of the remaining republican elements in Spain. But they were long self-exiled, so they lost touch with the day-to-day struggles of the Filipino people; they were unaware of the fact that their agitation for reforms, participation, and representation had already penetrated many of the remotest villages in the islands. Moreover, Spain, like the other countries in Europe, was undergoing a bloody turmoil; the republican government was overthrown and the monarchists came into power again. These two sudden turns of events, spreading diametrically from each other and irrevocably irreconcilable, antiquated their program and made it obsolete in the face of the new situation.

But the spirit of the period found full expression in the two powerful novels of Jose Rizal. *Noli Me Tangere,* published in Germany when Rizal was twenty-six, was an exposé of the atrocious conducts of the church and the state in the Philippines. Here for the first time, when it was treasonable to use the word "liberty," was a book revealing to the Filipinos that their rulers came, not to cultivate and guide their potentialities as a people toward a flowering, but to exploit the abundance of their natural wealth and to corrupt their innate spirituality. *El Filibusterismo,* published two years later in Ghent, is a political treatise severely attacking the Spanish regime. While it lacks the literary qualities that permeated the first novel, it gains in its hammerlike blows against the flagrant chicaneries of the church and the shady maneuverings of the state. It broke the opening wedge for the masses to lose faith in the cabalistic mission of the church and its amplitude, the altruistic nature of Spanish colonial policy.

The first novel translated from the Spanish into English under the title *Social Cancer* reveals that Rizal believed "the Filipinos had the right to grow and develop and any obstacles to such growth and development must be removed gradually under suitable guidance." In this, however, he was merely expressing the opinions of contemporary liberal Filipino leaders for reforms, participation in the government, and representation in the Spanish Cortes. This was his conviction also when he returned to Europe after observing personally the growth of Spanish tyranny in the islands; then he came to realize that not only political but also social reforms must be planned, if the growing rupture between Spain and the Philippines was to be avoided. And this is the theme of his second novel, translated into English under the title *Reign of Greed*. But there is a new element in the book: a deep sense of frustration confounded by an anarchistic idea to arm the people.

Rizal's loss of faith in reforms and his consequent confusion were the aftermath of his visit to the Philippines, where his compatriots' and his own agitational works in Europe were already translated by native leaders into the fabric of their undivided struggle and common good. However, hoping that a peaceable arrangement could still be effected between Spain and the Philippines, he forsook fiction and directed his energies to historical work. He edited and also annotated the only and earliest history of the Philippines—*Sucesos de las Islas Filipinas* by Antonio de Morga—an honest account of the Philippines in pre-Spanish times. He revealed in his series of articles, "The Philippines a Century Hence," that the Philippines, geographically speaking, was within the sphere of the surging American imperialist expansion; so it was absolutely necessary for Filipino leaders to study the history of the United States, and to schematize therefrom their fight for independence in order to be able to cope with the inevitable twists of history. The only answers to his persistent pleas for an enlightened relationship between his people and the rulers were the deadly bullets fired into his back when he was executed for treason by the Spanish government. But nothing was treasonable in his acts, works, and life. His execution was only the hysterical reaction of a crumbling despotism.

Thus Spanish sovereignty over the islands sounded its own death knell. The Philippine Revolution broke out under the leadership of Andres Bonifacio, a self-taught, self-disciplined stevedore at the port of Manila, backed up by his underground organization called the *Katipunan*. Membership in this organization was widespread, and the revolution was national in scope and had its main resource in the people. The Spanish regime fell after nearly a year of sanguinary warfare and the Philippine Republic was proclaimed. Under this government one of the most humane documents was written and approved.

The wreckage of revolution and the delicate problems of reconstruction split the leadership of the provisional government into two warring factions. Bonifacio, backed by his faithful *Katipuneros,* lost in the election of the first president of the Philippine Republic. General Emilio Aguinaldo, who was commander-in-chief of the revolutionary forces, won the presidency. This denouement gravitated to the final overthrow of Bonifacio and his shameful assassination, and to the eventful supremacy of General Aguinaldo who took command again, when, due to a misunderstanding with Admiral John Dewey, a war began between the United States and the Philippines.

However, the Philippines produced one of the finest intellects in Apolinario Mabini, who was prime minister under General Aguinaldo's presidency. He was the intellectual guide of the revolution, now that Rizal was dead, and the leading thinker of the constitutional convention called by the provisional government. Mabini, a paralytic and a self-educated man, is the Filipino counterpart of Thomas Jefferson. He was deported to Guam when the United States conquered the Philippines, in defiance to the oath of a subjugated people; but he complied with the request of the American government by writing the history of the Filipino-American War in English, a language he learned in exile.

From Balagtas to the American colonization of the Philippines there was a continuous tradition of intellectual rebellion against the hampering of native cultural development. Besides Balagtas, Rizal, M. H. del Pilar, Lopez-Jaena, and Mabini, there were also those who rebelled not only for cultural freedom but also for economic and political liberty.

Among these courageous intellects were Pelaez, Burgos, Panganiban, Luna, Bonifacio, Jacinto, Palma, I. de los Reyes, Apostol, and Pardo de Tavera. Moreover, these were the men who shaped and gave direction to the revolutionary heritage of the Filipino people.

Now the Philippines was under the United States. The revolution was broken. The leaders were either in exile or in jail. Some were dead. Those who were still in Europe gradually lost contact with native leaders. Another century had come and a new twist of history turned westward to the Pacific, heralded by American imperialism, embracing fanwise all islands in its swirling wake. The remaining leaders of the old generation were scattered, but another generation was born to taste the tyranny of a new regime. It was after all a labyrinthine circle of revolutionary upsurge and temporary defeat.

There followed long years of reconstruction and readjustment. The native cultural movement was disrupted and the richest elements of its character were destroyed by the new colonizers. The linguistic homogeneity that had been incorporated in Spanish was uprooted by the English language, and the dialects of the people succumbed one after the other without any favorable effects on the invading or invaded culture. All that had been tested for national growth, each tribe contributing to the common cultural fund, was relegated to a secondary function in the anarchy of new values. It seemed that the culture which was indigenous to the people and the land had become obsolete in this, the latest interpretation of native aspirations and life.

Dollar diplomacy prevailed, and with it there burst forth a superficial understanding of Philippine history. This was a novel purging of the red corpuscles, common to the imperialist countries of the west, from the bloodstreams of the people. Filipino writing was a sophomoric imitation of inorganic American writing, technically backward and utterly limited to the expression of sentimental middle class ideals. The Filipino middle class and petty bourgeoisie, as they had done under the darkest period of Spanish domination, came out again with their wealth and influence to collaborate in the administration of American colonial policy. Their latest collaboration gave birth to a new class: the government officials and the military, since the Filipinos were given partial and then full participation in the affairs of the government and the army. This was followed by the rise of the compradors or merchants, and the middle man, a liaison group that acted as contact and an advisory board for the petty bourgeoisie and top government officials. And this again was accelerated by the cooperation of the professionals, especially those engaged in law and jurisprudence, which had become the measure of success in the new act of values subtly imposed by American imperialism.

But the people, the peasants and the rising proletariat—what were they doing all this time? Back to their fields and factories, back to their villages and grass houses. Back to their wounds and scars, to their poverty and diseases. Yes, back to their broken lives to contemplate on the grandeur of a once glorious dream of national freedom and the nobility that crowns the brows of men. Back, back to their roots and soil, germinal again for another decade of plowing and sowing. Alas, that they had to undergo another generation or two of confusion and suffering.

After more than three decades of American influence, through various social, political, and economic changes, native writing commenced to nourish a positive cultural revival. This was the resurgence in the thirties of Filipino writers who took up where their predecessors left off in the cultural chain; they outlined a national program and compacted alliances with progressive writers' movements abroad. Inspired by the social consciousness of American writers who had awakened to the dangerous cross-currents in international politics, Filipinos began to examine their cultural heritage and to utilize its fundamental idealism in the awakening of a national consciousness. They directed a righteous indignation against the "culture-mongers" and social parasites that culminated in the creation of a broad organization of progressive writers.

A critical reevaluation of native culture appeared under the leadership of the younger writers and won support from government sources. Philippine literature perceived the importance of native folklore; it devoted a concerted effort to universalize education and to relate culture with political liberty. Spanish and American cultures were fusing and melting with the native culture, creating a rich and genuine Philippine synthesis. Filipino writers went back to their social roots—

the peasantry and the proletariat—and began to weave the threads of their folklore with the national tradition. It was only then that cultural activity became a national consciousness, spreading simultaneously with the growing industrialism.

When the Filipinos enjoyed more economic security and political freedom their potentialities emerged and demanded full expression. Therefore, the social awakening of workers and farmers were supplemented by the emergence of vigorous talents. The body of writing from this period, due to improved political relations and better economic opportunities, was suffused with new national hopes and ideals. Filipino consciousness emerged into a world of unlimited intellectual possibilities; it found configuration in poetry and the short story, which sprang from the depths of Philippine life Athena-like, full grown, generous and abundant. From these branches of literature, converging in time and space, the new cultural revival was to draw positive nourishments for a national flowering.

My Education

I came to America sixteen years ago from the village where I was born in the Philippines. In reality it was only the beginning of a tortuous search for roots in a new world. I hated absentee-landlordism, not only because it had driven my family from our home and scattered us, but also because it had shattered the life and future of my generation. This system had originated in Spanish times when most of the arable lands and navigable waters were controlled by the church and powerful men in the government. It came down [through] our history and threatened the security of the peasantry till it became a blight in our national life.

But now that I was in America I felt a vague desire to see what I had not seen in my country. I did not know how I would approach America. I only knew that there must be a common denominator which every immigrant or native American should look for in order to understand her and be of service to her people. I felt like Columbus embarking upon a long and treacherous voyage. I felt like Icarus escaping from prison to freedom. I did not know that I was coming closer to American *reality*.

I worked for three months in an apple orchard in Sunnyside, in the state of Washington. The labor movement was under persecution and the minorities became the natural scapegoat. Toward the end I was disappointed. I had worked on a farm all my life in the Philippines, and now I was working on a farm again. I could not compromise my picture of America with the filthy bunkhouses in which we lived and the falling wooden houses in which the natives lived. This was not the America I wanted to see, but it was the first great lesson in my life.

I moved to another town and found work on a farm again. Then again I moved to another farm town. I followed the crops and the seasons, from Washington to Oregon to California, until I had worked in every town on the Pacific Coast. In the end I was sick with despair. Wherever I went I found the same horror, the same anguish and fear.

I began to ask if this was the real America—and if it was, why did I come? I was sad and confused. But I believed in the other men before me who had come and stayed to discover America. I knew they came because there was something in America which needed them and which they needed. Yet slowly I began to doubt the *promise* that was America.

If it took me almost a decade to dispel this doubt, it was because it took me that long to catch a glimpse of the *real* America. The nebulous and dynamic qualities of the dream took hold of me immensely. It became the periscope of my search for roots in America. I was driven back to history. But going back to history was actually a return to the early beginnings of America.

I had picked hops with some Indians under the towering shadow of Mt. Rainier. I had pruned apples with the dispossessed Americans in the rich deltas of the Columbia River. I had cut and packed asparagus in California. I had weeded peas with Japanese in Arizona. I had picked tomatoes with Negroes in Utah. Yet I felt that I did not belong in America. My departure from the Philippines was actually the breaking of my ground, the tearing up of my roots. As I stayed longer and searched farther, this feeling of not belonging became more acute, until it distorted my early vision of America. I did not know what part of America was mine, and my awareness of not belonging made me desperate and terribly lonely.

The next two years were like a nightmare. There were sixteen million unemployed. I joined these disinherited Americans. Again I saw the rich fields and wide flat lands. I saw them from the top of a passing freight train. Sometimes I saw them from the back of a truck. I became more confused and rootless.

I was sick with despair. I was paralyzed with fear. Everywhere I went I saw the shadow of this country falling. I saw it in the anguish of girls who cried at night. I saw it in the abstract stares of unemployed workers. I saw it in the hollow eyes of children. I saw it in the abuses suffered by immigrants. I saw it in the persecution of the minorities. *I heard some men say that this was America—the dream betrayed. They told me that America was done for—dead. I fought against believing them. Yet, when I was socially strangled, I almost believed what they said about America—that she was dead.*

I do not recall how I actually started to identify myself with America. The men and women around me were just as rootless as I was in those years. I spent the next two years reading in public libraries. How well I remember those long cold nights of winter and the months of unemployment. Perhaps the gambling houses that opened only at night with one free meal for everybody—perhaps reading at the libraries in the daytime and waiting for the dark to hide my dirty clothes in the streets—perhaps all these terrible humiliations gave me the courage to fight through it all, until the months passed into years of hope and the *will* to proceed became obdurate and illumined with a sincere affinity for America. Finally, I realized that the great men who contributed something positive to the growth of America also suffered and were lonely.

I read more books, and became convinced that it was the duty of the artist to trace the origins of the disease that was festering American life. I was beginning to be aware of the dynamic social ideas that were disturbing the minds of leading artists and writers in America. I felt angry with those who fled from her. I hated the expatriates in Paris and Madrid. I studied Whitman with naive anticipations, hoping to find in him an affirmation of my growing faith in America. For a while I was inclined to believe that Whitman was the key to my search for roots. And I found that he also was terribly lonely, and he wrote of an America that would be.

I began to wonder about those who stayed in America and suffered the narrowness of the society in which they lived. I read Melville and Poe, who chose to live and work in a narrow world. I became intimate with their humiliations and defeats, their hopes and high moments of success. Then I began to hate the crass materialism of our age and the powerful chains and combines that strangled human life and made the world a horrible place to live in. Slowly, I was beginning to feel that I had found a place in America. The fight to hold onto this feeling convinced me that I was becoming a growing part of living America.

It was now toward the end of 1935, and the trade union movement was in turmoil. The old American Federation of Labor was losing power and a new union was being born. I started to write my own impressions of America. Now I was beginning to give meaning to my life. It was a discovery of America and myself. Being able to write, now, was a personal triumph and a definite identification with a living tradition. I began to recognize the forces that had driven many Americans to other countries and had made those who stayed at home homeless. *Those who went away never escaped from themselves; those who stayed at home never found themselves.*

I [was] determined to find out why the artist took flight or revolted against his heritage. Then, [while] doing organization work among agricultural workers, I fell sick with a disease caused by the years of hunger and congested living. I was forced to lie in a hospital for more than two years. Now, all that I had won seemed irrelevant to my life. Here I was dying—six years after my arrival in America. What was wrong? Was America so dislocated that she had no more place for the immigrant?

I could not believe that the resources of this country were exhausted. I almost died in the hospital. I survived death because I was determined to convince those who had lost faith in America. I knew in convincing them I would be convincing myself that America was not dead.

The Civil War in Spain was going on: it was another factor that gave coherence to the turmoil and confusion in my life. The ruthless bombings of churches and hospitals by German and Italian planes clarified some of my beliefs. I believe that this intellectual and spiritual participation in the Spanish conflict fired in me a new vision of life.

It was at this period that the Congress of Industrial Organizations came to power in industry. At last its militant stand in labor disputes re-invigorated me. Some of my democratic beliefs were confirmed. I felt that I had found the mainsprings of American democracy. In this feeling I found some coherence and direction and the impulse to create became more ardent and necessary.

America's most articulate artists were stirring. They refused to follow the example of those who went into voluntary exile and those who stayed at home and were angry with America. They knew that they could truly work if they stayed near their roots and walked proudly in familiar streets. They no longer created alone. They framed a program broad enough to cover the different aspects of their needs and abilities. It was not a *vow* to write for art's sake.

I found a new release. I reacted to it as a sensitive artist of my generation without losing my firm belief that America was happy and alive if her artists were happy and alive. But Spain was lost and a grand dream was lost with her. The equilibrium of the world was dislocated, and the writers were greatly affected by the setback of democratic forces.

I tried in the next two years to work with the progressive forces. But some of the organizations dribbled into personal quarrels and selfish motives. There were individuals who were saturated with the false values of capitalism and the insidiousness of their bourgeois prejudices poisoned their whole thinking. I became convinced that they could not liberate America from decay. And I became doubly convinced, as Hitler seized one country after another, that their prejudices must be challenged by a stronger faith in America.

We were now moving toward the end of the another decade. Writing was not sufficient. Labor demanded the active collaboration of writers. In the course of eight years I had relived the whole course of American history. I drew inspiration from my active participation in the workers' movement. The most decisive move that the writer could make was to take his stand with the workers.

I had a preliminary knowledge of American history to guide me. What could I do? I had read *Gone With the Wind*, and saw the extent of the lie that corrupted the American dream. I read Dreiser, Anderson, Lewis, and their younger contemporaries: Faulkner, Hemingway, Caldwell, Steinbeck. I had hoped to find in these writers a weapon strong enough to blast the walls that imprisoned the American soul. But they were merely describing the disease—they did not reveal any evidence that they knew how to eradicate it.

Hemingway was too preoccupied with himself, and consequently he wrote of himself and his frustrations. I was also disappointed with Faulkner. Why did he give form to decay? And Caldwell, Steinbeck— why did they write in costume? And Odets, why *only* middle-class disintegration? Am I not an immigrant like Louis Adamic? Perhaps I could not understand America like Richard Wright, but I felt that I would be ineffectual if I did not return to my own people. I believed that my work would be more vital and useful if I dedicated it to the cause of my own people.

It was now almost ten years since I had landed in America. But as we moved rapidly toward the war with Japan, I realized how foolish it was to believe then that I could define roots in terms of places and persons. I knew, then, that I would be as rootless in the Philippines as I was in America, because roots are not physical things, but the quality of faith deeply [ingrained] and clearly understood and integrated in one's life. The roots I was looking for were not physical but intellectual and spiritual things. In fact, I was looking for a common faith to believe in and of which I could be a growing part.

Now I knew that I was living in the collective era. Where was I to begin? I read Marxist literature. Russia was then much in the minds of my contemporaries. In the Soviet system we seemed to have found a workable system and a common belief which bound races and peoples together for a creative purpose. I studied Russian history as I had studied American history. I tried to explain the incoherence of my life on the grounds that I was living in a decaying capitalist society.

Then we felt that something was bound to happen in America. Socialist thinking was spreading among the workers, professionals, and intellectuals. Labor demanded immediate political action. For the first time a collective faith seemed to have appeared. To most of us it was a revelation—and a new morning in America. Here was a collective faith dynamic enough to release the creative spirit that was long thwarted in America. My personal predicaments seemed to vanish and for the first time I could feel myself growing and becoming a living part of America.

It was now the middle of 1941. The dark clouds of war were approaching our shores. Then December 7 came to awaken a decadent world. Japan offered us a powerful collective faith which was pervasive enough to sweep away our fears and doubts of America. Suddenly I began to see the dark forces that had uprooted me from my native land and had driven me to a narrow corner of life in America. . . . At last the full significance of my search for roots came to me, because the war against Japan and Fascism revealed the whole meaning of the fears that had driven me as a young writer into hunger and disease and despair.

I wrote in my diary: "It is well that we in America take nourishment from a common spring. The Four Freedoms may not be realized in our times but if the war against Fascism ends, we may be sure that we have been motivated by a native force dynamic enough to give form to the creative spirit in America. Now I believe that all of us in America must be bound together by a common faith and work toward one goal. . . ."

Freedom from Want

If you want to know what we are, look upon the farms or upon the hard pavements of the city. You usually see us working or waiting for work, and you think you know us, but our outward guise is more deceptive than our history.

Our history has many strands of fear and hope, that snarl and converge at several points in time and space. We clear the forest and the mountains of the land. We cross the river and the wind. We harness wild beast and living steel. We celebrate labor, wisdom, peace of the soul.

When our crops are burned or plowed under, we are angry and confused. Sometimes we ask if this is the real America. Sometimes we watch our long shadows and doubt the future. But we have learned to emulate our ideals from these trials. We know there were men who came and stayed to build America. We know they came because there is something in America that they needed, and which needed them.

We march on, though sometimes strange moods fill our children. Our march toward security and peace is the march of freedom—the freedom that we should like to become a living part of. It is the dignity of the individual to live in a society of free man, where the spirit of understanding and belief exist; of understanding that all men are equal; that all men, whatever their color, race, religion, or estate, should be given equal opportunity to serve themselves and each other according to their needs and abilities.

But we are not really free unless we use what we produce. So long as the fruit of our labor is denied us, so long will want manifest itself in a world of slaves. It is only when we have plenty to eat—plenty of everything—that we begin to understand what freedom means. To us, freedom is not an intangible thing. When we have enough to eat, then we are healthy enough to enjoy what we eat. Then we have the time and ability to read and think and discuss things. Then we are not merely living but also becoming a creative part of life. It is only then that we become a growing part of democracy.

We do not take democracy for granted. We feel it grow in our working together—many millions of us working toward a common purpose. If it took us several decades of sacrifices to arrive at this faith, it is because it took us that long to know what part of America is ours.

Our faith has been shaken many times, and now it is put to question. Our faith is a living thing, and it can be crippled or chained. It can be killed by denying us enough food or clothing, by blasting away our personalities and keeping us in constant fear. Unless we are properly prepared, the powers of darkness will have good reason to catch us unaware and trample our life.

The totalitarian nations hate democracy. They hate us, because we ask for a definite guaranty of freedom of religion, freedom of expression, and freedom from fear and want. Our challenge to tyranny is the depth of our faith in a democracy worth defending. Although they spread lies about us, the way of life we cherish is not dead. The American dream is only hidden away, and it will push its way up and grow again.

We have moved down the years steadily toward the practice of democracy. We become animate in the growth of Kansas wheat or in the ring of Mississippi rain. We tremble in the strong winds of the Great Lakes. We cut timbers in Oregon just as the gold flowers blossom in Maine. We are multitudes in Pennsylvania mines, in Alaskan canneries. We are millions from Puget Sound to Florida. In violent factories, crowded tenements, teeming cities. Our numbers increase hunger, disease, death, and fear.

But sometimes we wonder if we are really a part of America. We recognize the mainsprings of American democracy in our right to form unions and bargain through them collectively, our opportunity to sell our products at reasonable prices, and the privilege of our children to attend schools where they learn the truth about the world in which they live. We also recognize the forces which have been trying to falsify American history—the forces which drive many Americans to a corner of compromise with those who would distort the ideals of men that died for freedom.

Sometimes we walk across the land looking for something to hold on to. We cannot believe that the resources of this country are exhausted. Even when we see our children suffer humiliations, we can not believe that America has no more place for us. We realize that what is wrong is not in our system of government, but in the ideals which were blasted away by a materialistic age. We know that we can truly find and identify ourselves with a living tradition if we walk proudly in familiar streets. It is a great honor to walk on the American earth.

If you want to know what we are, look at the men reading books, searching in the dark pages of history for the lost word, the key to the mystery of living peace. We are factory hands, mill hands, searching, building, and molding structures. We are doctors, scientists, chemists, discovering and eliminating disease, hunger, and antagonism. We are soldiers, Navy men, citizens, guarding the imperishable dream of our fathers to live in freedom. We are the living dream of dead men. We are the living spirit of free men.

Everywhere we are on the march, passing through darkness into a sphere of economic peace. When we have the freedom to think and discuss things without fear, when peace and security are assured, when the futures of our children are ensured—then we have resurrected and cultivated the early beginnings of democracy. And America lives and becomes a growing part of our aspirations again.

We have been marching for the last one hundred and fifty years. We sacrifice our individual liberties, and sometimes we fail and suffer. Sometimes we divide into separate groups and our methods conflict, though we all aim at one common goal. The significant thing is that we march on without turning back. What we want is peace, not violence. We know that we thrive and prosper only in peace.

We are bleeding where clubs are smashing heads, where bayonets are gleaming. We are fighting where the bullet is crashing upon armorless citizens, where the tear gas is choking unprotected children. Under the lynch trees, amidst hysterical mobs. Where the prisoner is beaten to confess a crime he did not commit. Where the honest man is hanged because he told the truth.

We are the sufferers who suffer for natural love of man for another man, who commemorate the humanities of every man. We are the creators of abundance.

We are the desires of anonymous men. We are the subways of suffering, the well of dignities. We are the living testament of a flowering race.

But our march to freedom is not complete unless want is annihilated. The America we hope to see is not merely a physical but also a spiritual and an intellectual world. We are the mirror of what America is. If America wants us to be living and free, then we must be living and free. If we fail, then America fails.

What do we want? We want complete security and peace. We want to share the promises and fruits of American life. We want to be free from fear and hunger.

If you want to know what we are—We are Marching.

Filipino Writers in a Changing World

Since the passage of the Philippine Independence Law in 1934, a resurgence of cultural activity has been spreading with the growing industrialism. The awakened consciousness of the workers and the farmers is supplemented by the emergence of new and vigorous talents in the various fields of literature. The political and economic developments are creating new hopes and ideals; it is a positive restatement of the ideals and hopes that found expression in the revolutionary period of Philippine history.

To stimulate the spreading cultural activity, a group of native writers formed the Philippine Writers' League. The primary objectives of the League are: To raise cultural standards; to fight for the democratic right to education; to cultivate a friendly contact with writers in other countries; to defend political and social institutions that make for peace; to protect the freedom of expression; and to create an alliance for cultural defense between writers and progressive forces.

So, aside from a basic cultural activity, the League is also active in the struggle for more democracy and civil rights. But the inducements and facilities for a professional literary life are still sadly lacking. Therefore the League, in compliance with a constitutional provision which provided for a governmental encouragement of letters, lately sponsored a literary contest embracing the three important languages in the Philippines: English, Spanish, and Tagalog. The results of the contest are so significant and historical that President Manuel L. Quezón of the Commonwealth government was obliged to announce a permanent literary contest.

The winning novel in English (Juan Cabreros Laya. *His Native Soil*. Manila. McCullough Printing Co. $1.25) is an important historical document because it marks the continuation of a literary tradition started by Francisco Balagtas in Tagalog and by José Rizal in Spanish. Only forty years in the Philippines, English has become a dynamic weapon in the hand of the young author who, using the rich scenery of his own childhood and the shifting intellectual life of his generation, is able to recreate and reflect the rapidly changing political and social attitudes of the Filipino people.

The winning volume of short stories (Manuel E. Arguilla. *How My Brother [Leon] Brought Home a Wife*. Manila. Philippine Book Guild. $1.00) is equally significant and important in the present campaign for an objective nationalism. Nearly all the stories are about workers, peasants, common folks, and city proletarians. What makes the collection a distinctive piece of literature is, aside from its lyrical and cadenced prose, the healthy and felicitous closeness of the people to the earth. So close are they to the Philippine soil that you feel the immortality of the earth itself in their speech and ways of living.

The winning volume of essays (Salvador P. López. *Literature and Society*. Manila. Philippine Book Guild. $1.00) is the most significant of all because, besides its deeply felt and sincere warning of the inevitable appearance of the powers of darkness in the Philippines if vigilance for the democratic spirit is not solidified, it is at once a constructive criticism and a positive affirmation of life. In this volume you find the old faiths and ideals beautifully illuminated with the new faiths and ideals, reflecting in a purely imaginative language the creative energies of the Filipino people, their high hopes and tragic hesitations, their magnificent endowments and fearsome denials. Here is a young man who is aware of the function of literature in society, who does not write for art's sake when the very foundations upon which the arts must stand are shaken and endangered. Here is a writer who feels the spirit of understanding and of belief in every man; of understanding that all men are equal; that all men, whatever their color, race, religion, or estate, should be given equal opportunity to serve themselves and each other according to their needs and abilities.

The winning volume of poems (R. Zulueta da Costa. *Like the Molave and Other Poems*. Manila. McCullough Printing Co. $1.00) reveals a healthy feeling of internationalism among the younger generation. One is reminded of the democratic spirit of Walt Whitman, his sincere call for equality among all peoples and races in America—yes, Whitman's cry to go back to history for materials and inspiration, to know and to affirm the fertility of the native soil. The portentous climax of the volume is the poet's glowing invocation to José Rizal, the national hero, who is the personification of all the hopes and ideals of the Filipino people.

It is not hazardous to predict the future of Philippine literature, judging from the results of the first contest. But the life and the future of the Philippines depend on the outcome of the present political and economic crisis in the Orient. However, the increasing interest of Filipino writers in modern American literature and in the literatures of other countries is definitely bridging an alliance that neither war nor racial differences can destroy or blot out.

The Filipino writers are beginning to study the history of their people. They are beginning to draw inspiration from their native soil. They are beginning to create an attitude which is the most necessary factor in the growth of a great native literature—a definitely sharpening attitude which the new conditions manifested in the consciousness of the younger writers. And more, they are beginning to feel the tramp of marching men, the tearing down of obsolete institutions in some countries, and the creation of new forms of government in others.—*Los Angeles*.

I Am Not a Laughing Man

I am mad.

I am mad because when my book, *The Laughter of My Father*, was published by Harcourt, Brace and Company, the critics called me "the Pure Comic Spirit."

I am not a laughing man. I am an angry man. That is why I started writing. I guess you will have to be angry at something if you want to be a writer.

I will tell you how I became a writer. Perhaps you will find something in my story that you can use when you write, maybe an idea or an inspiration. Perhaps you will be so mad with me that you will start to write. And that is what I would like you to do.

Well, it started with the war. I was working at a fish cannery in San Pedro, California, when it came. Then my friends started going away, some to the armed forces and others to wartime industries. I was lonely. This was the beginning of my anger.

Then my right hand was paralyzed; perhaps a relapse induced by the cold water where I washed the fish heads at the cannery. I could not work fast any more. I was fired. This time my anger took a definite shape, not that I had not been fired before from other jobs. I was fired many times and in many places.

I packed up my things and went to Portland, Oregon, where a friend of mine had written me about a job at a hotel. But he had left for Alaska when I arrived. I wanted to follow him because there was work at the fish canneries but the last boat had left. I was mad.

I wandered in the streets. I went to several hotels looking for the job that my friend told me about. I slept in the bus station at night. I was ready to shake the world when a California farm labor contractor found me eating a stick of gum for lunch and peanuts for dinner. Well, he asked me if I would like to go to Seattle with him and be his publicity man.

Why not? Salary—it was not mentioned. Hotel accommodation—it was not mentioned either. So what? I had the assurance of three meals a day. I could sleep in his car at night—but I don't sleep much anyway. I could walk in the streets when he was using his car and go back to work early in the morning.

I was supposed to write articles inducing the cannery workers in Alaska, when they came back to the mainland, to go to California, which was badly in need of agricultural workers. Well, I was so mad when I arrived in Seattle that I wrote 35,000 words in three days which went into leaflets, newspapers, and brochures.

It was hard work all right. I nearly lost my eyesight on the third day. When you are before the typewriter for three days the machine becomes an illusion and the sound which the keys make is like a faraway circus music that returns to your memory interminably, when you bump your head on the table or when your cigarette burns your lips. But my employer, inspired by my industry, put me in a hotel. And now I started working hard because I was really mad.

Why didn't he give me this nice room before? I looked out the window and watched the barges and small boats sailing up and down Puget Sound. At night I put out the lights and sat in the dark listening to the deep melancholy sound of the foghorns. Then something infinitely delicate sprung up in me, like a little seed that breaks ever so gently to give forth a life in the world. Perhaps it was like a bird that wakes up from its sleep, flutters endlessly, wanting to fly into freedom.

That was it. I felt restless. I was not contented with my work; there was something big that I would like to say. My publicities worked, because the cannery workers proceeded immediately to California. I should not be angry. But I was angry with myself—angry because I did not know where to begin. I guess you must have a beginning to begin something really big.

I had quit my job and had left the hotel when my opportunity presented itself. A literary agent in New York wrote me about trying to write a text for Norman Rockwell's "Freedom from Want," one of the FOUR FREEDOMS which he was illustrating for the *Saturday Evening Post* and the Treasury Department. I rented another room and wrote the article in two hours, that mad I was with myself because I did not know what to do.

Five days later I received a telegram that the *Saturday Evening Post* bought my article for nearly a thousand dollars. Then I was really mad. Why didn't somebody tell me that it was easy to make money in America? Why did everybody let me suffer and starve? I was not only mad with myself but with everybody around me.

I packed up my things again and returned to Los Angeles. I gave away my old clothes and shoes. I paid my debts. I gave away part of the check I got for my article. In ten days I was stranded where I had started: no money, no job. I wrote to a Federal agency in Washington about placing me in one of its various writing departments.

The men in Washington surely took their time. The answer did not come for a long time. While waiting for it, I wrote 100 poems in three days. But when the answer came at last, I had already rearranged several of the poems for an organization in California that gave me a little money, and the book was published by Coward-McCann under the title *The Voice of Bataan*. Some of the other pieces went to magazines here and in England.

So I had reasons to be angry with the government men for not answering me promptly.

Now it was winter and the money I got for my poetry was gone. I went to Stockton, California, hoping to work in the asparagus fields (where a Filipino worker makes $25 a day for two months). Unfortunately I could not find a crew to work with because I was not fast enough. It was my right hand again, and I was mad because while a common Filipino laborer was making $25 a day I was not making anything.

I went to town and started writing short stories at the back of the farm labor employment office. I wrote three or four stories a day, in one sitting, stopping only to eat or drink coffee. When I went out at night I mailed the stories to New York.

Several days afterward *The New Yorker*, a magazine I had not read before, bought several of my stories. I was mad. What kind of publication is this that bought my stories for a fabulous sum? I went to an old magazine shop and bought 100 back issues of *The New Yorker* hoping to read them. But it was so cold that I had to wear my overcoat, hat, and gloves when I wrote. Then, angry with the cold, I started burning the old copies of *The New Yorker*, because my left leg started swelling.

I wrote like a man racing with death and in fifteen days produced 75 stories. *Town & Country* bought several stories. And then *Harper's Bazaar*.

I left the cold office in Stockton and returned to Los Angeles and spent all my money.

I did not want to look for a job any more. I was through with that. I wrote to several publishers in New York reminding them of my stories in the magazines and the numerous pieces I had in my room. Would they care to look at them?

But I did not have to write to them. At the same time that I was writing my letters the publishers were also writing theirs reminding me that they would like to see my manuscript. So it was a happy coincidence after all. Harcourt, Brace & Company sent me a telegram, beating the others by a day. So I sent them a selection of my stories. In a few days a contract and an advance of $500 dollars came, and once again I started spending like a millionaire. Why not? There was plenty of money in America. When I needed money I could always sit down for two hours and dash off a story.

When *The Laughter of My Father* came out, I was angry because everybody laughed reading it. I was angry when I wrote it in the back room of a cold office. But the readers did not know that. I arranged a few more and sent the manuscript to my publishers. So when *My Village Was Enchanted* (which is a companion volume to *The Laughter of My Father*) comes out, I hope the readers will remember how angry I was when I was writing it.

Now I had more than I could spend. I had paid all my debts. I had a new suit. Once again I felt the little seed stirring inside me. I took a train and went to a little town in Iowa, not knowing that it was a dry state.

Then I was really angry. I did not know what I would do with my days and nights. My friends were fighting for me. They were working for me in the defense industries. What could I do for them? What would this kind American woman who took me to her home think of me?

I did not want her to think that I was a bum. Not that I don't like bums. I like some of them; there are many kinds of bums. I made a little table in the yard and started writing my autobiography. In 28 days a 600-page manuscript was finished. I packed up my things again and went to New York and showed it to my publishers.

They wanted to publish it right away. What a life! Here I was, not yet thirty, and already a 600-page autobiography!

So at last, in late December, my autobiography—*America Is in the Heart*—will be published to tell the world that I am not a laughing man!

I guess that is why I started writing. I was angry. And I was sore at a guy named Saroyan and another named Wolfe. Who do they think they are anyway? Wrote a play in two days because he was sore at the world? Wrote millions of words on top of a frigidaire because he was afraid he could not tell everything in his life span?

I was sore at them, all right. So I wrote like mad, too, as though we were in a duel.

I guess that's the way it is with me. You try it sometime. Get sore at some guy. Or get sore at me. Remember that I came to this country as a common laborer—that I have no formal education whatsoever. I am sure you will sit down and write furiously.

I am sure you will say: "Who does he think he is anyway?"

The Writer As Worker

Why should I write about labor unions and their struggle? Because a writer is also a worker. He writes stories, for example, and sells them or tries to sell them. They are products of his brain. They are commodities. Then again, a writer is also a citizen; and as citizen he must safeguard his civil rights and liberties. Life is a collective work and also a social reality. Therefore the writer must participate with his fellow man in the struggle to protect, to brighten, to fulfill life. Otherwise he has no meaning—a nothing.

Now culture being a social product, I firmly believe that any work of art should have a social function—to beautify, to glorify, to dignify man. This assertion has always been true, and it applies to all social systems. But always art is in the hands of the dominant class—which wields its power to perpetuate its supremacy and existence. Since any social system is forced to change to another by concrete economic forces, its art changes also to be recharged, reshaped, and revitalized by the new conditions. Thus, if the writer has any significance, it should write about the world in which he lives: interpret his time and envision the future through his knowledge of historical reality.

And these are times that demand of the writer to declare his positive stand—his supreme sacrifice—on the question of war or peace, life or death. The writer who sides with and gives his voice to democracy and progress is a real writer, because he writes to protect man and restore his dignity. He writes so that this will be a world of mutual cooperation, mutual protection, mutual love; so that darkness, ignorance, brutality, exploitation of man by another, and deceit will be purged from the face of the earth.

A writer should be political also. Government or states are always in the hands of the ruling classes, and so long as there are states, there are also tyrannies. In a bourgeois state, under capitalism or imperialism, the tyranny is against the working class, against the majority. . . .

Filipino writers in the Philippines have a great task ahead of them, but also a great future. The field is wide and open. They should rewrite everything written about the Philippines and the Filipino people from the materialist, dialectical point of view—this being the only [way] to understand and interpret everything Philippines. They should write lovingly about its rivers, towns, plains, mountains, wildernesses—its flora and fauna—the different tribes and provinces. They should write about the great men and their times and works, from Lapulapu to Mariano Balgos. They should compile the unwritten tales, legends, folklore, riddles, humor, songs, sayings. They should illustrate that there was a culture before the Spaniards uprooted it. When these are written, they should extenuate and amplify. The material is inexhaustible. But always they should be written for the people, because the people are the creators and appreciators of culture. . . .

The making of a genuine artist or writer is not mysterious. It is not the work of Divine Providence. Social conditions, history, and the people's struggle are the factors behind it. My making as a writer and poet is not mysterious, neither was I gifted by an unknown power. It was hard work and hard living. Suffering, loneliness, pain, hunger, hate, joy, happiness, pity, compassion—all these factors made me a writer. Plus, of course, my tenderness, my affection toward everything that lives. Plus, again, my participation in the people's fight for peace and democracy.

I did not know any writer until I had three books published. Some writers are reluctant to [reveal] which writers influenced them. I probably read most of the greatest novels, plays, short stories, poetry of many nations, but those who influenced me most are Americans, French, and Russians. In particular, Balzac, Jack London, and Maxim Gorky. But mostly Gorky in the novel and the drama, Nicolas Guillen and Pablo Neruda in poetry, and the Marxists in literary criticism. If you have ever lived in one of the slums of the U.S., I know you would also be influenced by it. I lived in the slums of Los Angeles, and I never escaped its terrors, its soul-sickening atmosphere. . . .

I don't care what some writers in the Philippines think of me. That is their privilege. But I care about what they write, for or against war, for or against life.

Poems

Biography

There is no end of sadness.
When winter came and sprawled over
The trees and houses, a man rose from
His sleep and kissed his wife who wept.
A child was born. Delicately the film
Of his life unfolded like a coral sea,
Where stone is a hard substance of wind
And water leaking into memory like pain.
He was a young man. He looked at himself
Through a glass that was too real to image
His face, unreal before his eyes. These were vivid
To the hands; these were too real
To the hearts that bled to sustain life.
He was a man. And the sun that leaped
Into his eyes, the grass beneath his feet
That walked cobbled streets, the cities—
All were a challenge to his imagination:
But his mother decaying in a nameless grave,
And his father watching a changing world
Through iron bars, his broken childhood,
Were as real as pain locking memory.

Surely the Living Departed

because I found him giving his eyes away
for a dying relative who might have been my father
he opened doors that I had forgotten
and I explored obediently to my own sorrow

he came with the face of my brother who died
in his private honor believing in words
and the promises of words that haunted me
and I took the face because it was mine
but the passage was too small for my sorrow
and the rooms were full of guns

I rushed to the light and called for my comrades
I called for the saints and for one who was beautiful
in the world where war was unknown
but he led me to the door of departure
and raised a hooked hand and took the eyes from me
those eyes that might have been my father's
and surely I wanted to stay in the darkness
where the beauty of death was not the sorrow

The Manifesto of Human Events

The huge stage was there and already
the neon signs were illuminated
and these were the words—"LOVE REIGNS
SUPREME IN PEACE   HAPPINESS IS FIRST
IN INDIVIDUAL FREEDOM"—

          We sat
behind the great curtains waiting,
but the gunmen came and wrecked
the place in the dance of our fears.

Now we hold a neatly folded hope.
When they come again with murder in their hands
nobody can stop us from touching a gun
nothing can keep us from throwing a bomb.

Blood Music, 1939

The serpent's quick tongue, the lark's sharp
Flight against flashing sunlight, surrendering
All that space relates to suspended time—

And we listen to the marching feet approaching.
We sit in the cold room waiting. We look out
Into the streets fearing. Only little boys parading
With innocent feet, drilling to the drums beating
The sharp notes of discipline and order;
Only little men preparing for war and death.
And we are trembling. But here is familiar sight,
Common ground, known faces, tall trees leafing. . .

The rocket's flare in the heart of night,
Compelling sleep to leap into the wake
Of tragic moments, shattering all peace—

And we hide in the cold room, silencing
All words of protest, praying for morning
To come out of the sudden red rioting.
While headlines are screaming war, squadrons
Of aeroplanes pouring liquid fire of destruction,
And bloody dictators flashing arms, and broken
Promises, threats and ultimatums, and empires
Shaking in the sudden conflagration of death. . .
We listen to the drums beating blood music.

The Shadow of a Tear

And the vision torn asunder . . .
The twelve-year-old girl waiting in the dark . . .
How the banker will sleep tonight, contented
With his swelling willing young mistress.

"Did I cry when they took my
mother away? When the old judge
coddled me in the back room upstairs?
I could have cried but did not.
I was born with tears in my eyes.
God died the day I was born."

Hey, you, do you remember me?
Look at my face. Do you see the sign?

But the words signify numerous things
That neither you nor I can comprehend.
These nipples of bombs and submarine designs,
All the earth's murderous cry. All lying.
Reassemble the vision and form a star.
Be immuned from tears while the guns burst
In the littlest thing alive, merest flow. . . .
The waiting future seems so long ago. . . .

Death and Transfiguration

This is the land. These are the people.
Trees are full under fine starlight.
Fields are bright with drooping wheat.
Heaven, heaven. Paradise in whose mountains
The heart leaps to higher desires: the return
To simple childhood and moonlight, the power
Of dreams and nightmares, the joys of sin . . .

This is the city. These are the buildings.
The long streets are empty tonight.
The lamps die with the dead of midnight.
And the tenements are dark. *Cold, cold.*
I feel every moment that moves to blind
The heart with sadness, and slowly, softly
Turns the flaming mind into solid stone.
No man is free when life is a fragment
Of a dream whispered by a dying woman . . .

The hours move. Noiselessly the night
Escapes the terror of emptiness. Coldly
The poor cry in hunger under breaking snow.
From the window I move to reach the years
For the one moment in whose ageless chain
My wishes flame like full wheat under moonlight.
Soon the day will break and show our crimes.
And nothing can stop the million voices;
Not till this land and these people
Rise and conquer the loneliness together.

Waking in the 20th Century

The night shifts with the summer blue of the
ocean and the horizons turn like a lifted cup.
There are stars in the sky. My feet are on the ground.
I walk in the warm wind and my heart is beating. . .
Like the waves upon the shore, where motorists are
making noises and conflagration of light. The night
is like a trembling heart, beating louder and louder
to the distant murmur of planes and artilleries . . .

I waited in the night and now it is near dawn.
The image of a new world lifts its shorelines
under fading stars, deep in the drinking blue.
I am caught by a spasm of sadness and fear . . .
As the day breaks, the flood of the world's
miseries congeals me. I see my father as he was
in those years, huddled behind the wooden plow,
the rainstorm rearing about him. A little man
hoping for the quiet of sun, and abundance . . .
A transport plane takes off and now it is a leaf
in the cloudless sky. Once more I am jerked
to the present, and found the death of myself.
I am chilled by the death of unborn children,
the bonfires of history, the lost unwritten songs.
I see the unfinished experiments destroyed,
and the whole of life stirring in blood.

The day is like a trembling heart. Alone
in the harbor, I feel the world burst
in the wide canyons of my thoughts . . .
I am glad I have seen everything

For there will be days when we will stand together
Fighting for our right to stand together,
I think they will understand why we should
Stand together in our time.

Letter in Exile

Hourly the planes scour the skies to chart
The uncharted defenses of their loved country.
It is summer and the waiting steamers will
Unload by the sounding sea, to fill the needs
Of cities falling in the hunger of working men;
While the green hills widen their luxuriant
Shoulders of sharp glades, caught in the palm
Of the determinate sun, born of the islands.

All seems to concentrate on their way.
They make millions and their sons enter night clubs.
Bright virgin girls moan and bleed in their beds.
They close banks and their daughters throw money
To titled foreign gentlemen and cynical waiters.
Their bourgeois homes are wrecked. Into the streets
They pursue the course of their passion. They hold
Life in bubbles of drunkenness and fancy.

Knowing the tremendous web of this mistake,
I think of our favorite little islands
Cupped in those dovelike moving seas,
And our paternal homestead where exuberant
Brothers and silent sisters met every morning
To exhibit all ways of courtesy.
We were passionate in those days. Our parents
Condoned no dishonesties and personal indecencies.

Recalling all this before the hour of midnight,
I remembered you, brother, and hoped you
Could watch with me the splendid glide
Of limousines in this street, and in that other,
The long parade of hungry working men

That approached my window at dawn to remind
Me once again of the coughing orbit of life
In this strange land, their loved country.

We didn't have the poet's vision or the hangman's
Dream to twist the whole of living on our finger,
But in those islands, under familiar trees we spoke
Of the littlest things with the simplest joys.
There were no books and hard intellectual thoughts,
But we grew into manhood with the music of trees
In our hearts that would not break, breaking
At last to the barrenness of hard city streets.

All of it was anxiety. All the years that passed.
And I am still facing a greater anxiety;
The promised happiness that never came to me.
Ten years for me and twelve for you, and that other,
The other younger brother who could not find himself,
Fifteen years—and he was only a child when he came.
But we are still here burning with a thousand fevers,
Though now more discerning, the enemy close at hand.

I was God's wonder boy: but if I did not
Defile the greed of mad men, if I did not save
Beauty from the naked blasphemies of money,
You must know that I cried when the Jews
Were driven from their country, when the Negroes
Were burned in their homes. You must know
That with these feeble hands I crept to the window
Unashamed to die in a world gone mad with power.

Power and greed will ravage beauty and give us
Loneliness. But all this will come to pass.
So live the New Year flooding the city with noises,
Like the tragic noises of revolution, that reach me
Like a heartstroke. And all will move forward
On the undiscriminate course of history that never
Stops to rectify our tragic misgivings and shame.

Portrait with Cities Falling

This is the shadow of the unexpected hour.
As I walk across the tight room to breathe
The thin fog coming in from the strange night,
As I sit on the rocking chair to watch the key
In the lock turn twice and stop and turn again,
The shadow moves like a solid body and divides
Into multitudes of crosses, one upon the other,
So that the hands loom like the curling tentacles
Of a gigantic seamonster about to strike a prey.
I am pursued by the shadow. Everywhere I go
I see ghostly hands moving. I lie sweating
At night, hearing creeping hands in the darkness.
If I sleep, I am haunted by evil dreams.
If I wake, I imagine monstrous ills.

I open the door and I see a man without eyes.
But his hands are enormous, they reach everywhere.
And his feet are millions, they march everywhere.
At a distance, he is a man; when I look closer,
I see a woman reclining with starlight in her face,
Who is like any woman living or dead, only, only
Her hair is like the rainbow, multicolored, reaching
Everywhere with the sure quickness of the lightning.
And under dropping stars, her bigness is humanity.
A profusion of burdens, a Magdalen of men.

Sing like violinstrings. In the flowing darkness
The streetlamps flutter. The poor hug their hunger.
I am waiting, waiting. Soon the sun will be up . . .

Will they bear arms, will they come killing,
Will the headless man and the starlight woman,

Will they come together with the ancient emblem,
Will the lonely boy come with them, will they come,
Will they destroy the crosses across the profound years,
Will they come, I among them, I who have waited
Nameless in history, who will remember the hour,
Will they come to remake the world—?

The moon dies across the continent.
The wind screams and something lives.

For a Child Dying in a Tenement

How hard it is to see you go;
to watch the shame of starvation in your face.

Dear child, you are among the first to know
the terror of plenty, the crimes of innocence,
the anguish of poverty . . .

             I guess I know
the cold of winter, the despair of being poor,
the terror of loneliness and of not having fun.
I guess I know the perplexed look in your face,
the unanswered question, the wordless answer;
all the faces that could not stand pain.

Fear is dying. Now try to sleep off
the agony of hunger, the lion in the hollowed breast,
the spreading fire snapping the walls of the lung.
You are among the first to go. Now try to sleep.
And now goodbye till we meet again.

The Foreigners

You cannot blame us. We followed the sun
And the rain with gladness and hope.
There are many lands to go to,
But we are astounded by your horizons,
And we are glad we came with our children.
We came to share with the machinery of your greatness,
But we are unhappy to discover this:
Your people are miserable from the lack of mutual speech,
And their children are stereotyped.
We cannot be like them—
We brought our country's speech with us.

I am afraid I cannot write our language,
But I can work and walk in the streets
Peopled with men who know no compromise,
Till I stumble against you in the dark;
And I can rap at you and scratch you like a cat,
And I can make you feel the strength of our city.

We can jump over the tall buildings like leaves
But without words to deceive us,
And fall upon your feet
But without tears to deceive us—
We are invincible with death!
Look and examine us!

Needing No Time

Needing no time for mourning over
Vanished splendors, the future receives
Us into its inner reality where
The movietone of memory is a mimicry
Of gleaming cities and other discoveries;
Where the past is a sunset of pale clouds
Consumed by history now buried in the ages.
We stand in the sunset and gawk at the sun,
Choking ourselves with our dusty cries.
We want the past to jump into our pockets,
We want to jingle it at our pleasure, knowing
That this is the way life clings to love,
This is the way faith comes to life—
A perfume spreading in the spreading day.
The flight of hours into the years tells
Us that the past is a heap of burned leaves.
And we cannot have it with empty hands
Clutching at the fugitive winds of earth,
Cannot want in our march into the morning.
The past is past, and we cannot remake it.
If we cannot remake it, we do not need it.
If we do not need it, there is nothing to fear.
If there is nothing to fear, it is worth destroying.
The future is for hoping, and we want it.
If we want it, we can have it.
If we can have it, it is all.
If it is all, it is worth fighting for it.
This is the way we face the coming day.
This is the way we stand in the sunset
And gawk at the sun, needing no time
For mourning in our march into the morning.

Hymn to a Man Who Failed

Evening and the voice of a friendly river
The symmetry of stars, time flowing warm,
The perfect hour sitting on the tree-tops,
And peace, bird of shy understanding, waiting.

This is your world, this tin-can shack on the dry
River bed, this undismayed humanity drinking
Black coffee and eating stale bread, this water
Blue under the dark shadows of the proud city.

Lie down and laugh your worries away,
Or sit awhile and dream of impossible regions,
While there is no hunger, no endless waiting,
No cry for blood, no deceptions, no lies.

You are lost, lost between two uncertainties,
Between two conflicts, the mastered and the unharmed.
You are altogether alone and cold and hopeless.
The end is crouching like a tiger under your feet.

Evening and returning home, finding no peace,
No embrace of devotion, my beaten friend,
O failure who returns always to the dry river bed,
We are betrayed twice under the fabulous city.

Factory Town

The factory whistle thrilled the atmosphere
With a challenging shriek; the doors opened suddenly
And vomited black-faced men, toil-worn men:
Their feet whispered wearily upon the gravel path;
They reached the gate and looked at each other.
No words—lidless eyes moved, reaching for love.
Silence and fear made them strong, invincible, wise.
They shook their hands and tossed their heads back
In secret defiance to their fragmentary careers,
And paced the homeward road with heavy hearts.

These were the longest years of their lives;
These were the years when the whistle at four o'clock
Drove them to the yard, then they scurried
Home heavy with fatigue and hunger and love.
These were the years when the gigantic chimneys blocked
The skies with black smokes that reminded passersby
Of a serpent-like whip of life within, bleeding,
Scarred with disease and death. These were the years . . .

Faces behind the laced doors and curtained windows,
Did you see the young man stand by the factory gate,
His face serious and forlorn, brittled with pain,
His hands unsteady with nervousness—did you see him?
Look at the lengthening line of voiceless men waiting
By the factory gate that will never be men again.

Meeting with a Discoverer

And it came to pass that a new continent was discovered.
Pioneers cleared the wilderness, broke the plains;
a sweeping empire rose between two living oceans;
cities rose, monopolies rose: so now the ticker heart
appropriated the lives of millions, the future of millions:
the discoverers' sons were branded and deported
to strange lands that refused to receive them . . .

And in the course of this my year, before the planes
sunk Spain under a sea of workers' blood, swastikaed,
in the middle of my life a new discoverer came
and charted the island of my dreams and nightmares:
"In that land where you came from, do they sing songs?"
"Do they respect the women, protect the children?"
Not waiting, "Tell me everything because we are
the same. The discoverer in me wants to know what
strangers will become part of me." Eagerly,
"I carry the blood of many nations in my veins."
Then we looked at each other and shook hands,
inquiring no more.

But waking at midnight
to your troubled breathing beside me, I sat
in the darkness, in the night of centuries,
knowing that you carried in your blood my blood
that cried to be born within the bounds of history.
Something like tragedy but not grieving;
something deeper than desiring or living.

We are not pure in blood but one in living dead.

Biography Between Wars

There was no anger. The meadows spread
Filled with bubbles. And the stars on the snow
Swung toward the gulf; and the night was mortal.
And the trees in the wind were immortal . . .

                                    And he said:
All summer we sat in the sun. There were swallows
From the south and we drove them from the cornfield.
They flocked to the tall grass in the shade.
I slept in the hay, in the toolshed—

I climbed the falling embankment. I said:
Hold on tight; light is approaching the village.
Then I knelt on the snow, feeling the bullet wound
Under his arm . . . Then the planes swarmed like swallows
And ripped the night with lilies of screaming fire.

Like a curse it imprisoned us . . .
                            My husband died
In Teruel, she said, looking at the tenements.
I remember his laughter, I said, touching the child.
He was his father's dream to live, she said.
So long as the dream lives the death is dead, I said.

O foreigner, bound to the heartless years,
We watch for the dawn of loneliness and fears.
You, who from the soil looked forward to mortality,
Who marveled at the sea's quiet level,
And over all hoped for earthbound peace—
So long as the dream lives the death is dead.

If You Want to Know What We Are

If you want to know what we are who inhabit
forest, mountain rivershore, who harness
beast, living steel, martial music (that classless
language of the heart), who celebrate labor,
wisdom of the mind, peace of the blood;

If you want to know what we are who become
animate at the rain's metallic ring, the stone's
accumulated strength, who tremble in the wind's
blossoming (that enervates earth's potentialities),
who stir just as flowers unfold to the sun;

If you want to know what we are who grow
powerful and deathless in countless counterparts,
each part pregnant with hope, each hope supreme,
each supremacy classless, each classlessness
nourished by unlimited splendor of comradeship;

We are multitudes the world over, millions everywhere;
in violent factories, sordid tenements, crowded cities,
in skies and seas and rivers, in lands everywhere;
our numbers increase as the wide world revolves
and increases arrogance, hunger, disease and death.

We are the men and women reading books, searching
in the pages of history for the lost word, the key
to the mystery of living peace, imperishable joy;
we are factory hands field hands mill hands everywhere,
molding creating building structures, forging ahead,

Reaching for the future, nourished in the heart;
we are doctors scientists chemists discovering,

eliminating disease and hunger and antagonisms;
we are soldiers navy-men citizens guarding
the imperishable will of man to live in grandeur.

We are the living dream of dead men everywhere,
the unquenchable truth that class-memories create
to stagger the infamous world with prophecies
of unlimited happiness—a deathless humanity;
we are the living and the dead men everywhere. . . .

II

If you want to know what we are, observe
the bloody club smashing heads, the bayonet
penetrating hollowed breasts, giving no mercy;
watch the bullet crashing upon armorless citizens;
look at the tear-gas choking the weakened lung.

If you want to know what we are, see the lynch
trees blossoming, the hysterical mob rioting;
remember the prisoner beaten by detectives to confess
a crime he did not commit because he was honest,
and who stood alone before a rabid jury of ten men,

And who was sentenced to hang by a judge
whose bourgeois arrogance betrayed the office
he claimed his own; name the marked man,
the violator of secrets; observe the banker,
the gangster, the mobster who kill and go free:

We are the sufferers who suffer for natural love
of man for man, who commemorate the humanities
of every man; we are the toilers who toil
to make the starved earth a place of abundance,
who transform abundance into deathless fragrance.

We are the desires of anonymous men everywhere,
who impregnate the wide earth's lustrous wealth

with a gleaming florescence; we are the new thoughts
and the new foundations, the new verdure of the mind;
we are the new hope new joy life everywhere.

We are the vision and the star, the quietus of pain;
we are the terminals of inquisition, the hiatuses
of a new crusade; we are the subterranean subways
of suffering; we are the will of dignities;
we are the living testament of a flowering race.

If you want to know what we are—

WE ARE REVOLUTION!

To My Countrymen

With a stroke of my hand, I cut the tides
That swept the destinies of men.
Now in this field of combat, where my armies
Challenged the tragic course of history:
Look, listen: cries crescenting blood,
Crimsoning our island; because I came.
Here I slapped the earth to make you a home,
Confounding fate, even the farthest star,
Where light resolved itself into your faith;
Because I came to stake a claim on the world.
And across the flaming darkness of life,
I flung a sword of defiance to give you freedom:
Here in the seven-pillared wisdom-house of truth,
Where I knelt, where I wept, where I lived
To change the course of history; because I love you.

Correspondence

Letters (1937–55)

December 12, 1937

I often weep when I am alone because they [American women friends] show me so much tenderness and fidelity of friendship. Western peoples were brought up to regard Orientals or colored peoples as inferior, but the mockery of it all is that Filipinos are taught to regard Americans as our equals. Adhering to American ideals, living American life, these are contributory to our feeling of equality. The terrible truth in America shatters the Filipinos' dream of fraternity.

May 2, 1938

Do you know what a Filipino feels in America? I mean *one* who is aware of the intricate forces of chaos? He is the loneliest thing on earth. There is much to be appreciated all about him, beauty, wealth, power, grandeur. But is he a part of these luxuries? He looks, poor man, through the fingers of his eyes. He is enchained, damnably to his race, his heritage. He is betrayed, my friend.

April 27, 1941

I am sure of myself and what I can do in the world. Tonight, however, I doubt myself. . . . I know deep down in my heart that I am an exile in America. Every moment of time is a million years of hope. Every acquaintance is a departure from life. . . . I do not ask for love. No. I ask only for a small measure of happiness. . . . Love would only make it the harder for little guys like us to bear the unbearable terrors of life. Yes, I feel like a criminal running away from a crime I did not commit. And the crime is that I am a Filipino in America.

June 22, 1942

But as my body decays and slowly crumbles to uselessness, my mind becomes solid and crystallized. The most important thing for a young writer to have is health. Somehow I became convinced of the validity of some of my beliefs. . . . We think casually about the freedom of writing. There were centuries when writing was a crime punishable by death. There were times when intelligence was a serious crime. . . . In our exuberance, remember how we became privileged to think and speak and write.

July 22, 1942
In spite of everything that has happened to me in America I am not sorry that I was born a Filipino. When I say "Filipino" the sound cuts deep into my being—it hurts. It will take years to wipe out the sharpness of the word, to erase its notorious connotation in America. And only a great faith in some common goal can give it fullness again.

September 24, 1945
The war was still in its desperate days, and now it is all over. I have changed in many things both political and literary since then: there is no time to go back now. But I surmise that you have also changed, being an artist sensitive to your time. It is awfully hard for us who are artistically inclined, because the world to come will demand new ideals and attitudes. Perhaps our world to come was the one that went with the war: perhaps we can cope with the coming new world. I hope so. But we must be born again, I guess, to find a place in it. We must reconstruct our thinking and living in order to be of use in its realization. . . . My recent poetry reflects the agonies of a Filipino lover loving a white woman in America, using the racial conflicts in California as a background. Writing these pieces gives me anger, protest, bitterness, loneliness—and on the other hand love, passion, yearning, tenderness.

June 7, 1946
In spite of my growing fame and bank account, I am still besieged with a terrible feeling of aloneness. I believe the scars of other years are still in me, never to heal again because of the horrible havoc they have inflicted upon me both psychologically and spiritually.

It is a shame that the aridity of a Pinoy's [Filipino's] life and mentality is so deep and devastating that so many of us believe that it does not exist at all. It is no wonder that Rizal in Europe was like a leaf cut from the tree:

perfect in itself, as a leaf, but separate from the mother tree. In other words, it is almost impossible to trace his life and correspondence with other Filipino intellectuals in his time, and to evolve a continuous thread of his thoughts as he developed them into a personal philosophic interpretation of the world in which he lived. Yet he had lived in a rare age of Filipino cultural flowering, a socio-political renaissance unlike our own time where almost every Pinoy abroad and at home is seeking the easiest way out in petty politics and making a profitable living from a gangster economy. I am sure you can understand my predicament in these surroundings, especially here in America where the intellectual interests of our countrymen are abysmal and degrading.

October 26, 1946

I refuse to be in the company of corrupt Filipino leaders. I will make it my lifetime proposition to live away from them, to work in seclusion, and to be seen only with common laborers and other such people— which was the kind of person I was in the years long gone here in California, among the Pinoy farm workers and the domestic servants. Someday perhaps I will come out again, but only if I have really something significant to contribute to the general scheme of things in the Philippine scene.

January 6, 1947

I am just a writer who is trying to know more about his art and to use it in the struggle for a better society and a more enlightened mankind. I am not a good writer, I think, but I will try my best to strive toward a certain form of perfection: that is, a perfection of thought and style. Like most serious artists I believe that content and form are inseparable elements of good artistic creation: one generates the other, but both are generated by a noble theme of universal significance. I do not believe that art is alien to life: it is a crystallized reflection of life, deepened or heightened by our individual perceptions and sensibilities. . . .

March 12, 1947

There are things for us to do in America, in the name of our country, of course, though the word "country" has become obsolete. But this feeling is just the last residue of a nationalistic philosophy which we have acquired from our ancestors . . . but now the fight is for certain democratic principles, certain universal principles that belong to all mankind.

April 15, 1947
We are the only expatriates who really lived and worked with the people, and I'm very sentimental because of this fact. Sometimes I lose my historical perspective because of this sentimentality. But it does not really matter: human life is only a matter of four or five decades to normal people. And then we are dead, and then our arrogance, wealth, clothes, women are forgotten. But while we are all alive we must try to understand each other, give each other confidence, help, happiness and goodness.

Most of our contemporaries are turning to politics, to easy jobs, to betrayal of former ideals. And most of them don't know that I have no quarrel with writers as such, but the ideas they represent or fight for. I'm not even happy, like most of them, I don't even have a home, like most of them. And I don't even have a wife, understand? Yet they want to hate and hurt me—for what?

April 16, 1947
The making of a great cultural heritage is so closely associated with the lives of those who make it: then, surely, we should write about them in a warm and loving way so that other generations would think of the magnitude of, say, a great epic poem with the life and times of the author.

We should work like common people, absorbing, learning, remembering. It is only when we know the depth of the human soul, its tranquility and violence, its magnificence and fragility, that we are really capable of writing something of significance and importance in man's life. The magnitude of a creation of art (and other human endeavors) is measured by the suffering endured by the creator in the hour of its composition. The Philippines is undergoing a great tragedy: why are the writers not challenged by it?

June 25, 1947
I was surprised to discover how little I knew and understood about man and his mysterious universe, and on the other hand, how enormous is

humanity's accumulated knowledge and experience compared to mine.
. . . The Negroes' crystallizing struggle against the racial myth in this
country is gaining strength every day; because I find them a theory and
a course of action. I feel confident that my projected book on Rizal, if I
live to write it, will be my *magnum opus*—my gift and last will, in fact, to
the Filipino people. I think I understand all of Rizal now that I have
been away for nearly two decades, now that I too have suffered an inner
agony—the agony of conscience. . . .

September 24, 1947
It did not make me conceited that out of the slums and kitchens of
California, out of the fear and hatred, the terror and hunger, the utter
loneliness and death, I came out alive spiritually and intellectually!
Instead it has made me humble and serious in my relations with my
fellow men.

. . . I came back to California with a wonderful dream and the
proliferation of my output for a little while was amazing, then it stopped
suddenly because of a terrible sense of guilt and fear. But now I know
what I have done; I do not aspire for wealth or power; I never did. I only
want to expose what terror and ugliness I have seen, what shame and
horror I have experienced, so that in my work, however limited in scope
and penetration, others will find a reason for a deeper grievance against
social injustice and a higher dream of human perfection.

It is true that the atom bomb is like a Damocles sword on our
conscience; but its fearsome might is no cause for us to abandon the
centuried dream of man to achieve progress and civilization. It should
instead inspire us to work harder toward a united mankind and one
world. Beneath the ugliness is a stream of beauty that never dies; and
when that beauty dies, all that is human will die also. And since man is
here to stay—man, poor, poor man—the beauty in him will never perish
in spite of the terror and the ugliness. . . .

November 15, 1947
I have lived a dangerous, violent life, and because I did not learn from
the experiences of other men, I blindly thought that youth would last
forever. Now the illusions about many things are lost; yet how refresh-

ing and heartening to remember that once, immediately before and during the war, we lived a life that had almost no comparison. In that narrow hotel room in Stockton, in that cold office where we worked every morning, in those little bars where we drowned many little fears and other complexes, all, all the unfulfulled dreams and other galaxies of inferiorities: all have driven us close together from the unfriendly corners of America and compacted our hopes in our common rootlessness and loneliness. And yet, looking back, I would rather be back in the unchartered world again than in this one, where I am floundering alone and sick. I think I am a victim of most of the social ills and other neuroses of our turbulent times.

I have become a stranger to people. When I go out of my room and walk in the streets, I feel as if I have dropped from another planet. Everything has become strange and far away: even everyday conversation does not seem to reach me anymore. I see men and women working hellishly, and young people loving passionately, and little girls and boys growing up memorizing the names of distant stars; but these activities of humanity are meaningless to me. I would like to go back to that suspiring innocence in years long gone. It is dangerous for any man to live alone and to dwell in the delicate world of his mind.

December 31, 1947
Anyway, my brothers and I have kept our respect for each other to the end of our days, and somehow, as men, we have also kept our dignity in America. This in itself is no hollow triumph. When my brother is gone, I know that I must work hard at my task because I will find his spirit in every decent word that is said or written around me. I feel proud to be a member of the human race when there are men like him living on the earth. And I am not afraid anymore, in heaven or hell, or to die, because of his presence among us all.

. . . I am grieved because he is going away; but history has determined our lives, and we must both work hard for what we believe to be the right thing for the Filipino people. In this task we will find great sorrow and joy, but we will also find in it the crystallization of certain affinities that we have for each other, and the other will be enriched by our affection and search for the good and decent in man.

... Our task is to live and explore the very roots of life, dig deep into the hidden fountainhead of happiness; and when we die, at last, we must die accepting death as a natural phenomenon and believing also that life is something we borrow and must give back richer when the time comes.

It was a great world—all our youth and dreams—but we must part with them at last. Life is full of memories, bitter and sweet ones that enrich us and keep us living and searching for decent things in the hearts of men.

February 5, 1948
Once I wrote a brief but beautiful piece about that world of fantasy called "To a Time Far Away" and it made me cry because what prompted me to write it was a vivid remembrance of my father's voice calling me one morning, that echoed with a soothing urgency down the valley of home. I always write about that life beautifully, but when I take another background like the U.S., I become bitter and angry and cruel.

April 13, 1948
There was no such kissing of hands in the pagan Philippines [as alleged by some American textbooks]; that was merely the symbol of servility that grew up in the minds of modern Filipinos, brought about by the Church and the damning philosophy brought by the Americans that the white man is superior to the brown man. This is false, of course, because our pagan forefathers were brown men of superior ability and unvanquished manhood; men who, because they had come from a sturdy race and a superior civilization, never bowed to other men except in acceptance and giving of courtesy. It is bad to arouse any feeling of inferiority in the young; let them stand equal with the young of other lands.

Genius is not the sole property of one race or one class of men; and the possession of a soul which indicates the ability to appreciate the truth and beauty in all things belongs to everyone and to no one. That is why Carlos P. Romulo's books and most of all the other books written by Filipinos have failed as *Filipino* books: they fail to bring out the individuality of the Filipino mind, the shaping of that mind, its growth and possibilities; and finally they fail abysmally in pointing out the universality and resiliency of that mind. They fail to show that man is one, indivisible, sprung from one root. I think you understand what I am driving at now. But that is only one example. The men of the Philippine Revolution were never defeated; they were merely bludgeoned to surrender piece by piece for several reasons, such as the anarchy that grew up within their forces, the scandalous personal ambitions of some of the top leaders, and the terrible impact that modern industry and the army that the American forces had brought upon them.

May 6, 1949
Writing is a pleasure and a passion to me—I seem to be babbling with multitudinous ideas, but the body is tired and weak. . . . I would like to repeat what Rizal had done for Philippine literature.

November 2, 1949
I have a secret dream of writing here a 1,500-page novel covering thirty-five years of Philippine history, combining all the great qualities of these novels [books by Gorki, Tolstoy, and other European writers]. Of course, we will see . . . . I owe it to the Filipino people. But this is only one of a series of four novels covering 100 years of Philippine history. This one I am working on now covers 1915–1950. One will cover the period from the birth and death of Rizal. Another from his death to the outbreak of the first war. And the fourth will cover 1951–1961, which I consider will be a great crisis in Philippines history. And there you have the whole panorama of my project.

There is really a need for a novel covering the ideal friendship, courtship and marriage of a Pinoy and an American white woman, but the pressure for a novel about the Philippines at this stage of human civilization is demanding. And I am very sensitive to historical currents and cross-currents. I hope I am right.

December 1, 1949
I am not a scholar, neither have I any passion for historical research. What drives me is the force of the idea, the historical fact, the cultural vigil, the literary itch, and so many other factors innate in a writer.

January 8, 1950
I am sure you understand that I have tried to explain our cultural growth from a materialist point of view. That is why I have left out a good many fine writers who have specialized in their own fields, like Jose Garcia Villa . . . . In the kind of article I have written [see "Filipino Writers in a Changing World"] he deserves a line or two, but nothing more, since to me he does not represent the growth of *our* literature. Rather, he is a phenomenon, an artist who expresses a declining culture after it has reached its height; and his place is somewhat questionable especially in a literature which is just beginning among a more primitive people. He is somewhat in line with Baudelaire and Rimbaud, for these two appeared when French poetry had already reached its vortex and was on the downgrade. Naturally they were great apostles of the poetry of decay. When we speak of literature as a continuous tradition, a growing cultural movement, Villa is out of place and time.

What I am trying to do, especially in my writings since I left Stockton, is to utilize our common folklore, tradition and history in line with my socialist thinking. This is a dangerous path, more so, if you are a novice in this kind of thinking. But in the long run we are pooling our knowledge together for a better understanding of man and his world; not to deify man, but to make him human, that we may see our faults and virtues in him. That is the responsibility of literature and the history of culture.

March 21, 1953
Human life could truly be a paradise, in many respects, if the money spent for destruction were used for the elimination of disease, schools propagating tolerance, factories for necessary consumer goods, and research centers, clinics, hospitals, maternity wards, etc. In fact, we should have a Department of Peace in the Cabinet, instead of a Department of War. Hate, greed, selfishness—these are not human nature. These are weapons of destruction, evolved by generations of experimenters in the service of ruling groups, be it a tribe, a clan, a prince, a king, a democracy. These destructive elements have finally become so subtle, so intricate, so deeply rooted in men's minds in our time, the era of international finance, that many people sincerely,

though ignorantly, believe them to be the guiding forces of nature. Love, kindness, pity, tolerance, happiness, beauty, truth—these are the *real* human nature from which a galaxy of other relevant virtues spring, take root and flourish in manifold form—in what we call brotherhood or common humanity, as the ideal of honest men in the world.

And because of this cultivated ability, plus my enduring fidelity to enduring human virtues and their amplitudes in our everyday life, I can clearly see my place in the vast panorama of human struggle. What is this struggle? To live a little longer with the minimum of pain, close to each other in peace, and to contribute what we can toward the elevation of the human spirit. So short, so brief, so little is the infinite flame of life in all its forms—this is our life on this planet. Why do we hate and kill each other when we are going to die sooner or later? Where are the conquerors of yesteryear?

There is consolation in poetry, and also inspiration. But not in cynicism. . . . Now when I write anything I am always propelled by the main forces of life and society . . . and now realize the heroism of men to make the world a better, happier place.

June 2, 1953
In a public institution you have to contend with the aberrations of varied personalities; and the most damnable is the abysmal ignorance of what we call the masses of the American people. I don't want to be misunderstood: it is true that the American people are intelligent, democratic, and magnanimous; but these people belong to a minority. However this minority is vanguarding and illuminating our democratic heritage and thus pushing forward the march of freedom for the bewildered masses. And, if you could live in their midst, in a public institution, without lacerating your soul, then you would be the better person. You would in all probability learn to live as a less isolated human being. I am writing from experience, because I have been lucky to live, work and struggle with all kinds of races of people in America. It is disastrous to know and live and work and struggle only with intellectuals and professionals. They are a type apart from the masses of people: the size of their pocketbook is the real barrier; and the two classes cannot compromise on a common lasting allegiance.

To listen to a Scarlatti's violin solo, remembering a lost mountain village is a beautiful and tear-provoking experience: to watch hundreds of workers building the towering scaffolding of a new bridge—well, that is breathtaking and tear-provoking too. But it would be tears of joy, seeing the magnificence of man's collective labor.

You see, I have grown in the heart and in the mind. Never will I think one malicious thought about anyone living or dead. Every unexpressed thought will some day be discovered drifting with the elements of the air, when man's intelligence reaches an unbounded freedom to utilize its scientific discoveries for the spiritual advancement of humanity. This may happen in a millennium, but it will come. And when it does, man will be so great, so bursting with love for his fellow man, that I would like to be present to say to all: "I want to thank you for living with you in the same world."

Do I sound like Holy Writ? There are certain things in that Great Book for those who are capable of love, pity, compassion and dignity— and great loneliness, anxiety, sorrow, fear and uncertainty. I am fortunate—when I was ten years old a brother of mine gave me a copy of the Old Testament for a birthday gift, explaining in his unorthodox way that it was the story of a great people's struggle against tyranny, and in those long struggles they somehow conceived the beneficence and omnipresence of God, which was later distorted by men of little or no faith to suit their ambitions; a conception so new and magnificent and universal in appeal that it provoked the most atrocious barbarity from the rulers and hirelings, but also brought the most courageous and brilliant galaxy of intellects for the human race.

. . . Everywhere I roam I listen for my native language with a crying heart because it means my roots in this faraway soil; it means my only communication with the living and those who died without a gift of expression. My dear brother, I remember the song of the birds in the morning, the boundless hills of home, the sound of the language. . . .

January 7, 1954
I will try to tell you a short story: Once when I was a little boy in that village where I was born, I dreamed that we could remake this world into a paradise. In such a world there would be no darkness, no

ignorance, no brutality to man by another man. In such a world there would be no inhumanity, no indignity, no poverty. In such a world there would be no deception, no ugliness, no terror. In such a world there would be mutual assistance, mutual cooperation, mutual love. This is the dream which has sustained me down the terrible years, and it is with me still; only it is more lucid now, more terrifying in its vastness. I would like to give you a glimpse of this dream some day.

January 17, 1955
My making as a writer and poet is not mysterious, nor was I gifted by an unknown power. It was hard work and hard living. Suffering, loneliness, pain, hunger, hate, joy, happiness, pity, compassion—all of these factors made me a writer. Plus, of course, my tenderness, my affection toward everything that lives.

. . . I don't care what some writers in the Philippines think of me. That is their privilege. But I care about what they write: for or against war, for or against life.

April 8, 1955
My politico-economic ideas are embodied in all my writings, but more concretely in my poetry. Here let me remind you that *The Laughter* [*of my Father*] is *not* humor: it is satire; it is indictment against an economic system that stifled the growth of the primitive, making him decadent overnight without passing through the various stages of growth and decay. The hidden bitterness in this book is so pronounced in another series of short stories, that the publishers refrained from publishing it for the time being. . . .

Letters to an American Woman

June 11, 1937

Dear D.,

When you left the hospital I ate some of the candies and drank a glass of milk. You are kind to bring me these things, and if it is not for me, it is for the life of a man.

This morning I was reading FOMA and it shook me so much. I like Gorky's early works; the later books are not so strong as these. I shall be happy if you can bring me more. Gorky is great; it is very likely that he is a phenomenon, a kind of genius that has to appear in a country where he is almost needed. He was the product of turmoil in Russia, and his being a member of the oppressed classes signified that these classes alone could save the country from ruin. And they have; history will tell us that they can hold it. They have struck new directions, new magnificences for man. They will make mistakes, power will corrupt some, but the many will rise from their past. It is strange that so few average Americans know the history of this terrible oppression, or, for that matter, the history of our countries. They must learn.

And you must remember this: our country, or any country of the Western world, cannot produce a man like Gorky—raw, defiant, bitter, understanding, compassionate, beautiful—because the American people have to suffer deeply to know what life is like. I do not mean that misery should be a prerequisite for the production of great art. I think the greatest art will appear in a happy world of free men, but this new world will not come without pain and struggle.

I wish that our unhappy humanity had a common vision of a peaceful, creative future to hold in mind as a kind of beacon for hope and guidance in this warring world.

                                        Carlos

Dear D.,

How good it is to be strong enough to hold this notebook on my chest and write! I must rest often, but it is not so bad.

I am besieged by memories today. I am young and already I have lived several lives since my childhood in the islands.

Men look back to their childhood, especially when they are so old that they no longer have the faculties to penetrate the possibilities of the future, or even have the courage to examine the present. It is also characteristic of dying men to look back. Maybe this is my case, but I believe not.

I am not old enough to look back with nostalgia, but because I am away from home I have a longing for everything that was lovely and happy. It may be that I shall never again see my country, but I feel strong and powerful and immortal in the thought that I can still remember fragments of my childhood. I know that the years have somehow made me love my country more.

When I was young I was told of a story called "The Man without a Country," but I wonder whether men with a country realize how poignant it is to be without one. I have been in the United States for five years, and it seems that although I love this country as much as any native-born American, I shall always feel strange and lost and forgotten. I have often been lonely. But in my loneliness I like to console myself by remembering incidents of my childhood in the Philippines.

Today I want to write you about one of the incidents I remember most vividly.

When I was seven years old, my mother, two brothers, and two sisters moved from our farm to town so that the children could attend town school; but I remained on the farm with my father for four years and attended the village school.

I vaguely remember my father as a quiet man. When he was not working in the field he was at home repairing his tiny grass house. He was always doing something. Sometimes he would visit my mother in town.

Until the rest of the family left the farm, I was only half aware of my father's existence. After that I became very fond of him. When I was eleven an incident occurred that caused me to regard him forever after with love and pity.

One afternoon he received a letter. He put it in his pocket and walked away. He did not tell me what chores to do as was his habit, and I sensed that he was troubled. When I realized that he would be gone for the day I took my sling-shot and went to the river. At noon I returned home and ate some rice that my father had cooked the night before; then I put on my straw hat and went out to play.

A narrow ditch ran close to our house and flowed into the rice fields. The water was clear and calm. I took off my clothes and knelt in the water. The sun was hot on my back and I turned around and waded to a deeper spot. I sat down and the water's level was about a foot above my head. Underneath, everything was wonderful; it was like the rhythm of underseas.

After a while I got out and dressed. The sun was still hot so I rested under the shade of a tamarind tree. I looked up at the sky through the low branches and then leaped for the lowest branch and climbed. The tree was high. I climbed higher and higher, until I reached the top. I saw our carabao fighting with another carabao by the river. They rushed against each other and locked horns. I climbed down quickly and ran toward them.

I threw stones at the other animal but he was stubborn. Grabbing a long pole from the ground, I smashed it against their heads and finally succeeded in driving the intruder into a clump of bamboos. Our carabao was cut on the right side, between the horn and the ear. I wiped away the blood with dead leaves and soon he was cropping again. At sunset we started for home.

Night came and my father did not return. I was sleepy but I wanted to wait staying up. I must have fallen asleep because when I opened my eyes he was sitting by the window, stringing beans under an oil lamp. I crept up to him and touched his legs. He looked at me and tried to smile, but I knew that something was wrong. After he had put the beans in an earthen pot of boiling water, he came to me and placed his palm on my forehead.

"I'll take you to town tomorrow, *anak* [child]," he said.

"I don't want to go to town."

"You'll live with your mother and brothers and sisters."

Then he told me that the short strip of land we had been farming had been lost to a money-lender.

I suddenly felt closer to my father than I had at any other time. When I knew that he did not intend to talk anymore that night, I went downstairs and fed my dog.

The full moon was high in the sky. I walked toward the water trough and sat on a clump of grass. The water was dark and calm. I could see the white reflection of the moon and my shadow under it. The upturned shadows of trees and an expanse of endless blue shone in the luminous light.

I dipped my finger into the water and touched the moon. The water swirled and the moon broke into little pieces. The sky tumbled and the stars danced like frightened fireflies. The world swayed and zoomed into space. And the water was still again.

On my way to the house I stopped by the shed and threw a bundle of hay to the carabao. When he saw me he flipped his big ears. I ran my hand over his head; a big patch of coagulated blood had formed on the wound. As I walked away I could hear his crunching.

I went directly to bed. The bamboo mat was thin and rough. A soft wind blew through slits in the bamboo floor. My father was very still, but I knew that he was awake. For a long time I lay thinking in the night.

                                        Carlos

October 3, 1937

Dear D.,

At two o'clock this afternoon my brother, Aurelio, was here. As we often do, we thought of home and our childhood and reminded ourselves of the early chapter of our lives.

My brother spoke of his student days—the happiest of his life, so he said. He was a teacher in the Philippines; in the United States he is a common laborer. But he still has the old nobility and dignity with which he can varnish his soul. Sometimes I wonder if he is happier than I because he finds peace in every little thing he does. And I look at myself knowing there will never be peace for me.

My resurrection of the past has been different from his because I had neither a college education nor a peaceful childhood. But I remembered an unforgettable fragment of my childhood and I told him. The story took place when I was ten years old, and living with my father on the farm.

Some distance from our house was a clearing which my father and I had been cultivating. One night he told me that we were going to plant coconuts in the clearing, and a few days later when the nuts arrived by cart from our home in town, we hurried to do the planting. My father dug the holes with a crowbar and I dropped and covered the nuts with fresh earth. I marveled at his strength because I had barely finished covering a nut when he had dug a new hole. When I worked rapidly and reached him, I leaned against my spade and admired him as if he were a god. At intervals he stopped and wiped the sweat from his face and neck with the back of his hand. He said to me in his melancholy voice, "In seven years they will be bearing fruit. You will be seventeen, and you can go to Manila and enter college. You will be a lawyer!"

Then he worked rapidly again, and at sundown we gathered our tools and prepared to go back to the hut. When we reached our grass hut, my father prepared dinner, and I went to the village well to fetch water for our carabao, chickens, hogs, and dogs. When I returned the food was ready and we ate like two comrades. Soon after dinner we went to bed. My father slept soundly. I could not sleep; I kept thinking of our coconuts and my brothers who were in town going to school, to dances, while my father and I were working for them and their ambitions. I finally dozed off, happy with the thought that the first day of those seven long years was ended.

The day before I sailed for America, I returned to have a last look at the coconut groves. There they were, all green and lusty, waving their palms in the bright April sun as if they knew that I was going away forever. I wept. But my elder brother laughed at my tears because the coconuts were no longer ours.

Please, dearest D, don't ever leave me.

Carlos

Dear D.,

I received your letter and I want to answer some of the questions you raised.

First, I did not say that I have a passion for gambling. I said it was the easiest way out for me. I hate it as much as you do. I tell you I learn easily, and I could have been a great gambler if I had wanted to be a parasite and a cheat and a liar. If you had known me then you would have known that I hated it. But I didn't gamble during all my life in America. Let me explain—

When I landed in Seattle, I was met by a swaggering countryman, a dapper Filipino, who sold me to an agricultural labor contractor for $7.50. There were seventy-five of us, all under twenty-five years old, who were cheated this way. I worked for a month under this unforgettable deal. At the end of the month the contractor vanished one night with all our money. I starved on that farm; then I escaped to become a dishwasher: $7.00 a week. I ran away from this second job at the end of three weeks and starved again. I drifted to Santa Barbara where I worked for almost three months in a bakery. Then I came down to Los Angeles. I was out of work again. I found the members of the outer fringes of society: hoboes, tramps, gamblers, prostitutes, etc. I was absorbed by them. In spite of all that had happened I was still innocent. You should have seen how they protected me from sin and debaucheries. Because in Filipino society there is a by-path on which these "unfortunates" walk and often meet the "educated" ones, I soon discovered the college students, graduates, newspaper workers. Because one thing leads to another, I was soon thrown into one lap of radicals, progressives, social workers. I became one of them, not by adaptation but by gravitation—the general process from an ignorant farm worker, city worker, student, to a class-conscious individual.

Come to see me this week.

                                            Carlos

Dear D.,

Your recent trip up the coast made me remember an experience of one of my own trips. Two of my friends and I were driving to Portland, in an old Model T Ford. When we stopped at a gasoline station in Redding, a small town in northern California, we noticed a few husky men talking near the station. Two of them came over to the car and one asked, "Filipinos?" We answered yes, and then he said, "Well, this town is too good for you. Leave just as soon as you get your gas."

We asked why we had to leave. He looked at us with contempt because we had the temerity to ask. His hatred, which had been cold and hard, immediately became violent and loud. The expression of his eyes was strained and wild, and his hands gripped the door.

"Pay your gas and beat it, you goddamn goo-goos, or we'll fill you full of lead!" He slapped his bulging hip, and we knew the trouble was more than insult. These men were probably hired vigilantes; California was full of them then. We drove away slowly as if life did not mean anything to us, but we were all afraid. We were only peaceful young men and we wanted to keep our lives.

Such arrogance and brutality are not always received passively by my people. The Filipinos, like the Spanish, are impulsive and quick with the knife. Their readiness in defense has surprised some of their white brothers who have given insults without expecting any retaliation.

One day, before I came to the hospital, I was talking to a Negro boy about race prejudice and he asked, "But there isn't any prejudice against the Filipinos in this country, is there?" When I told him a few of my experiences he was surprised, believing that Negroes are the only persecuted race in America.

We who know prejudice sometimes have a tendency to believe that we are the ones most discriminated against. There were times when I have been sad and bitter and felt this way. Then I remember that there are thousands of others besides Filipinos who have had similar experiences—Negroes, Chinese, Japanese, and even native-born whites. And I begin to feel less alone, remembering these people, and those few Americans I have known without a trace of race prejudice.

You are one.

I am all right now that you are in the city again. Thank you for the fruit you brought me. I will look at its beauty before I eat it. Your hands held it.

Carlos

December 10, 1937

Dear D.,

I. Why do Filipinos dress like dandies?

First of all, when we came to the United States, we were young. We work hard if there is work; we are not married (immigration laws do not include our women, excepting a few under rare circumstances); we have no dependents, no family ambitions to occupy our minds. We are not admitted to any American recreations except theaters and some tennis courts. Therefore we buy clothes, cars, spend all our money on our friends or girl acquaintants. We are very fond of dancing.

II. Are Filipino laborers also dandies?

Yes, some of them. Filipinos who work on farms live this way: ten or fifteen rent a house and live together, crowd together, and the most popular among them will get in touch with farmers and secure jobs for the whole group. At the end of the month, they pool the expenses, every man paying as much as the rest. Or, sometimes a worker lives in a boarding house (Filipino or Japanese proprietors) and pays more than the ones who live in a house. The boys who share a house take turns in housekeeping, cooking, running errands, etc., and therefore spend less money.

In a city a Filipino lives in a hotel if he is a quiet, studious person like my brother. If he is a happy-go-lucky fellow he lives in an apartment with a friend or two, plays cards, has parties, plays music. Those Filipinos who do domestic work, who work in homes or apartment houses, usually have to live on the premises.

On the farm a Filipino gets up at five or six a.m., puts on his work clothes, eats breakfast, goes to work. While working he does not often think of work at all but keeps on talking about women, clothes, places. He comes home after five p.m., takes a bath, eats his dinner, puts on his best clothes, and goes to town: theater, pool hall, gambling dens, shadowy houses—it all depends upon the person.

A Filipino loves courting. Our courting is more formal, poetic, and romantic than is the custom here. Since there are few accessible women, he may go to a pool hall with his musical instrument and sing till morning. He likes to go places, to be with friends; he hates isolation.

In the city, a Filipino goes to work in his best clothes, no matter how menial the work. He usually carries his work clothes in a small satchel. After work he does not return to his room or apartment or shared house; instead, he goes to his friends' room, or to a restaurant, a gambling house, pool hall, or dance hall and does not return before midnight. Many go to read in the library. Many more do not.

City Filipinos are generally more aggressive than the farm workers. A Filipino working in a restaurant is likely to date one of the waitresses; if he works in a hotel he may win the heart of a roomer. If he works in a family, or more likely, for a couple without children, it is not unknown for him to have a love affair with the wife. I am not saying that this is all true, but it is as true as all general reports. Many people are lonely, some are merely bored and empty; and it is a fact that acquaintance with Filipinos at work often removes the ignorance of race prejudice.

There are also Filipinos who do not work at all: gamblers, dance hall gigolos, stool pigeons.

Aside from these, there are those Filipinos, few in comparison, who are seriously interested in labor and economic problems. Many of them like to dance, of course, and wear good clothes, but they are decent fellows and hard-working, who try to make their countrymen here realize the importance of organizing for better living and working conditions. Sometimes I get disgusted and think that my people are hopeless; then I am ashamed of myself because I cannot blame them for what they are. Society is to be blamed for most of the frustrations and distortions of man.

I am ashamed of myself too when I think of the students who came here with college degrees and dreams of working at their professions in this golden land. Of those Filipinos who worked and went to college here, even more naive and hopeful of change. Doors were closed. Their minds and abilities and talents may have been trained for professions, their hearts filled with love for America, but they had brown skins. This will not always be so, but men will have to earn and learn their way out of this stupid ignorance.

Most of the Filipinos I know have no intellectual growth and are without social understanding. In fairness, I suppose this is true of all peoples. They do not read, not that they cannot read, but they do not care for good books. Without reading, and with only hard work and good times and their abnormal social life here, many are dead inside. I cannot live without reading; I want to help my people.

Whenever I had an opportunity, I used to talk about world conditions and the forces of society, and the importance of understanding our world. I used to talk to them about books I had read; I told them the pleasure of these good books. I even recited poetry I thought they could understand; that, being near music, was sometimes successful. Usually, then, someone would play a guitar or a mandolin or a piano and we would all sing Filipino songs. I like to remember these times.

But much that I said seemed fantastic and illusory to them. Nevertheless, the most ignorant or dull or good-time fellow among them was not suspicious of learning or poetry, but admiring. You know yourself that the ordinary American is often suspicious of the man of learning and the artist.

When I found it beyond my friends' understanding, or completely outside their small sphere of interests, I had only to tell funny stories and make them laugh. But I told these stories with love because these young men, far the majority of them, were good men. And we were all thousands of miles from our islands, alone (without even our women) in a strange, and often hostile country. Much of what we were told about this country before we came is false, but much of it is true. Most of us will die here because we can work here, and when we can work we will make a life for ourselves. Man always makes a life for himself from whatever he has.

Ask me more questions. I will answer them. I like for you to be inquisitive. While I was writing this letter, the hours went by so fast that here comes the sound of the long "food wagons" going through the halls like trains.

Carlos

Dear D.,

Good morning! I have a surprise for you. Here is something I have been writing gradually, an actual experience during my first year in this country. I hope some day to include it in my autobiography.

Please write soon and tell me frankly what you think of this.

I do not know whether the town of ———, Washington, has improved since I was there. I remember when we Filipino newcomers arrived in the early afternoon of that summer day I felt desolated by its isolation and the aridity of its atmosphere.

Our farm labor camp, two miles from town, was a wretched group of five tiny ramshackle cabins, dwarfed under a grove of towering eucalyptus trees. I was assigned to one of the rear cabins in a lower bunk with fifteen other laborers. I don't know how these five cabins squeezed in one hundred men, but it was soon evident that our boss, Cornelio, a Filipino giant with bulging eyes and a brutish manner, was a practical fellow, a heartless profiteer.

That evening of the first day when he stood imposingly on the rough table in the mess hall declaiming for nearly an hour, I knew he was not to be trusted. (Later in California, I was to meet many such clever speech-makers among the Filipino labor contractors).

It was in this camp that I met the student, Leon. He was one of those precocious Filipino youths whose perspective awareness came into conflict with the drab harshness and rigidity of an environment contrary to his compassionate and idealistic nature.

One fine morning, a week before our work started, I was wandering lazily in the orchard when a fair-sized apple hit my head from behind. I wheeled about and there he was—laughing. Never before had I heard a man laugh with such artless gaiety as Leon.

"Are you hurt?" he asked in my native dialect.

"Of course!" I was laughing too.

"Do you see any stars dancing here?" He waved his right arm above his head.

Then I knew that I liked him; and he liked me.

We followed one of the longest rows. He had lived all over the west, he said. Chicago, post office; Los Angeles, gardener; Mercedes, Nebraska, sugar beet tapper. During these years, whenever he could, he went to night school. Now he was saving money for his Master's degree in literature. He spoke earnestly of his future.

Suddenly he asked, "You're one of the newcomers?"

It was not really a question; he knew I was a newcomer.

"Yes."

"Eighty newcomers in this camp. They came before you. All young and inexperienced—peasant boys, with no idea what will happen to them in America." Leon's mood changed; he spoke gravely, and his dark eyes were somber. "I look at them with pity, trying to visualize them ten years from now. My vision makes me angry. I want to shout to them what I see. But they have just arrived and their illusions of life in this country help them through experiences like the one here."

I was not listening any more; I was not interested to know the future. But I noticed that he used English words where their equivalent in the dialect was lacking.

The sun burned us and heat waves trembled on the treeless plain, making a vast mirage. And while I listened to Leon, to his words that wounded my heart, I began to wonder if there was no bright spark of life left in the world.

"Why are you sorrowful?" I asked.

"Why not?" he answered impatiently.

"Five years ago when I first came here, there were only ten Filipinos. We used to work with the Indians, who were numerous, and with some poor white families. We were well liked. Today we outnumber the native Americans in the apple orchards, the hop fields, the melon patches—in all these places we have taken their place. The reason?

Because we are cheap labor. Suppose the townspeople wake up one day and drive us out?"

"Would they dare do that?"

"Why not? When we have taken their jobs."

Then we discovered that we had walked far. We were at the edge of town and stopped at a grocery store for a sack of candies before starting back to camp.

Beyond the town, where three dirt roads forked, a gang of boisterous young boys taunted us with stones and sticks. I wanted to fight, but Leon grabbed my arm and told me to run. We ran into the orchard, avoiding the open view of the road. When we reached camp we related the incident to a few of the fellows and they were filled with excitement. They spread the news to their companions and a noisy discussion ensued.

One of the old-timers, a dour fellow, predicted, "This is the beginning. I see blood in this town."

The old-timers untiringly squabbled among themselves while we newcomers stood aside or sat patiently and listened. Their talk drifted from the present to reminiscence. They had countless stories to tell, all sad and pathetic. It seemed to me that these men had reached the end of creation—everything hopeful in life was ended, nothing good could happen to them any more.

The cook, a tired, gaunt old man, interrupted us. We filed into the smoky mess hall where two long rough tables were carelessly set with tin plates full of half-cooked rice and enormous chunks of foul-smelling meat. I sat next to a voracious Cagayano [native of Cagayan province] noisily shoving mountains of rice onto his plate, pouring down his throat rivers of soup as though he were eating for the last time. He bit the tip of his tongue and howled with pain. Food smeared the edges of his mouth, but he was indefatigable.

I glanced around the tables. Leon was at the far end of the first table, close to the kitchen door, eating slowly, taking his time. He was dignified, handsome. Now his expression was hidden and lost and far away. I shouted to him above the roar of our companions. He looked up from the tin plate and I was glad to see his gentle smile. I was reassured by it; we shared a quiet communion, I thought, in the din that enveloped us.

It did not take us long—ten minutes at the most—to scoop down the food. When we left, full and heavy, the mess hall was in shambles. We ran into the yard, scattering among the trees. A lad, blind in one eye, came out with a *kutibeng,* and another lad, long-haired, and long-toothed, sang a native love song. Both were sons of fishermen, natives of the southern part of Luzon, and their song had the haunting presence of the sea. One bold old-timer insisted on American jazz, but the others remonstrated because they were stirred with nostalgia by this song of their homeland.

I walked away from the crowd and found Leon sitting on a patch of dry grass at the back of our cabin. I sat beside him for a long time in the moonlight night, away from the melancholy songs of yesterday, away from all thoughts of yesterday. We sat together wordlessly.

When we got up to go, Leon gestured toward the others and said, "I give them to you."

I lay awake for hours, puzzling over what he had said, unable to sleep in the cacophony of snores that soared through the stifling cabin. In desperation I left my bunk and went outdoors to sleep under the stillness of the stars and the shadows of the eucalyptus trees.

December 9, 1938

Dear D.,

I feel like working again. I have reached that part of my autobiography where race prejudice became more aggressive and alarming.

Have I ever told you that I passed through an Oregon town and was arrested for being a Filipino? It was like this: Five others and I were driving in a car from California to Seattle when we were stopped on the border, beyond California. The highway patrolman pulled up beside our car.

"Are you Filipinos?"

"Yes."

"Follow me."

He took us to the police station, and the Chief, a fat, beet-red man, demanded twenty-five dollars from each of us. We refused to pay because we knew we had not done anything. They threw us in jail, two dirty bedless cells, and robbed us of our money, every cent. We were kept in this jail for one day and two nights without food.

When the jailer came with our clothes, he kicked one of my friends in the solar plexus for asking where our money was. Then we had to return to the border, escorted by two highway patrolmen who laughed at our plight. I will never forget how they treated us. I have gone back to that town twice, hoping to meet those men who treated us badly, but the town has changed immensely and improved. The members of the police force were new. I suppose there was a police shake-up and those ruthless creatures were eliminated.

And do you know what happened to my companions? One is serving a life sentence because he murdered a white man who molested his wife, a half-Chinese, half-white whore. Another is married to a white girl from the Dust Bowl who was betrayed by her father when she was twelve years old. This fellow and this betrayed girl are living in a small agricultural town in California. Another is a union organizer. He works in the fields for the union without pay, half the time sleeping under trees and not eating what he needs. One has a Ph.D. and cooks in the greasy kitchen of a cheap restaurant and is so lonely for a wife that he will take anyone. Another is a domestic worker in Los Angeles. What happened to me? I do not know myself.

Carlos

August 3, 1940

Dear D.,

I have often thought of writing you but I have been lazy. Some of our countrymen have been visiting us and I have not had much privacy for writing. However, I have thought of you and now I am going to do something that I promised you long ago: I am going to write in this letter about the Filipino and his place in America.

But first, how are you? When we talked on the telephone last week I thought your voice sounded as if you were tired.

How are you coming along with your projected plan for a book on the Filipinos? Perhaps this that I am going to write will help. I want you to understand the handicaps that cannot be surmounted, no matter how hard a Filipino may try.

Do you think that even a well-educated Filipino would be hired as a teacher, a secretary, a reporter? There are 35,000 Filipinos in California, and what of our future? We shall grow old here, a lonely, unmarried, exhausted race of men unless we take steps to improve our conditions.

You have heard the question asked: Why did the Filipinos migrate to the United States and why don't they return to the Philippines?

I read in an American history book that President McKinley prayed to God on the question of whether or not to take over the Philippines, and only when He assured him that it was a Godly act did he make the decision. And so we became the "little brown brothers" and by and by we received an invitation from some of our rich relatives to pay a "visit" but not to become a legal part of the great American family. Of course, we were only admitted as poor relations, but at that time we were naive, young and eager, and we dreamed of a life of opportunity in America. We were brought to California to work in the fields, and the majority of us have remained in the fields ever since. We were wanted as cheap labor and we are desirable only as long as we remain cheap labor.

We like America. We want to live and die here. Most of the Filipinos in America came from small towns or rural districts in the Islands. We live in the cities: Los Angeles, San Francisco, Stockton, New York. We begin to feel as if America is our country, not in a possessive way, and with no designing thoughts of bringing about an Oriental infiltration of the Pacific Coast. No. A man is not conscious of his first identification with a country of his adoption. After the initial shock of strangeness has subsided he settles into the routine of making a living and gradually what was strange assumes familiarity, becomes a part of daily life.

In the Pacific Coast cities, the streets close to the Chinese, Japanese, and Filipino sections are America to the Filipinos. Main Street in Los Angeles is a gaudy street of burlesque theatres, ten cent shows, pool halls, stores that sell cheap clothing, where poorly dressed people walk—drunks, prostitutes, tramps, degenerates. It is a street where genteel people go "slumming" to view a sordidness safely removed from their own lives. Filipinos walk on Main Street. A Filipino can walk on Main Street with more confidence, feel less alien, laugh and talk with his countrymen. He may work all week for white Americans, but on Sunday he is sure to see some of his friends on Main.

Thousands of Filipinos, the major part of those in California, work in the fields. True, the farms are mostly corporation owned, but this cannot prevent a man who works close to the soil from feeling attached to that soil. Work in the fields is back-breaking, but the well-tended crops are green and beautiful.

Filipinos work year after year in the fields in California, living in towns or cities during slack seasons. Sometimes there are strikes and they strike for better working conditions along with their American co-workers. Laboring in the fields becomes more than a means of earning a living. Field work is a part of the great American scene. Filipinos are a part of this scene. They are a part of America.

I hope to write you more letters about my countrymen because within twenty years these conditions will have changed, perhaps be forgotten except by a few. These workers will have grown too old or exhausted to make up the farm labor force in California. And then what of the condition of the Filipinos and of the labor problem? This is for the future to solve.

Adios for now,
Carlos

May 7, 1942

Dear D.,

I ought to tell you a brief history of my brothers. I have four brothers and two of them grew up before I was born. When I was a little boy, living with my father in the village where I was born, I heard from one of my cousins about my oldest brother. His name was Apolonio and he was a school teacher in the town where my mother and my other brothers lived together.

I never saw this brother except at a distance when I was on my way to

America. Years later I heard many interesting stories about him from Filipinos who had known him in California. But I remember this brother, not because of the blood relation I have with him, but because he is the only one of our family who returned to the soil where he had his roots. In fact, he is one of the few Filipinos in America to return to his native land. He married and returned to peasant life and years afterward became a prosperous farmer.

I wrote to him after I had been in America five years. Before that time I was too inarticulate to write what I found in California: the race prejudice and the exploitation of our countrymen.

One day in the summer of 1941, when I was in a little town near Santa Barbara, I became acquainted with a Japanese farmer who had known my brother. It seemed that they had worked together in Fresno, a town near Stockton. We arranged to meet at a grocery store that evening. We walked to his cabin three miles away. A mild wind passing through the low hills rose up between the sea and the wide fields.

Kota was farming a twelve-acre plot of land, and that summer he had planted sweet peas and the air was sweet with their fragrance. We sat at the back of his cabin, near a running irrigation ditch. A full moon glowed above the low moving clouds; I could see clearly in the drifting light a farmhouse a mile away. The night was quiet except for crickets singing in the grass.

Kota soon excused himself and went to the cabin. He returned with a jug of *saki*. He poured the wine into two wooden cups. We started drinking the Japanese rice wine. It was like going back to the beginning of my life in the little village.

"You like me to play and sing song?" Kota asked.

"Yes," I said.

He went into the cabin again and brought out a small *samisen*. He squatted on the grass and hugged the musical instrument. As his fingers moved gently across the strings, I was lost in a world of small and graceful sounds.

I drank the cupful of *saki* quickly because I wanted to forget that long ago I was with my father just as I was with this Japanese farmer, singing our native songs under the moonlight of my childhood.

I was remembering that this man had known my brother, the one I had never seen except at a distance when I made a sudden decision to go to America.

I was then living in another town, far from my brother's town, but his house was on the highway to Manila. When I went to Manila I saw him standing in a wide rice field with one of his sons. I waved my hands to him and he waved his hands to me, but he never knew that I was his brother and the little boy beside him never found out either.

Long afterwards, in America, I remembered him standing with his son in the rice field. As the years passed I became obsessed with the idea of going back. But it was physically and financially impossible to return to my native country. Now and then, I would board a bus and travel toward the towns in the northern part of California, passing through the towns where my brother used to live. Sometimes I stopped to talk with Japanese farmers; other times I stayed a few days in San Luis Obispo and went with the farm workers to the rolling fields on the hills that fronted the sea. I picked peas with them, remembering my brother and his closeness to the earth of home and of America.

But the war with Japan came, and I know now that my brother is dead. He probably died in his rice field, defending it against the invaders. For my brother was like that.

Now I will tell you about my second brother; his life was brief and intense. He left behind a story that made me cry when I was lonely in America.

His name was Silvestre. I never knew him when he was a young man but years later he and I were good friends. When he was sixteen he joined the Philippine Army. At that time we were very poor and my mother and I used to cut rice for other people, sometimes staying away in other towns for three or four months.

Once I was ill of fever. I remember lying on the bamboo floor one morning and hearing the sound of heavy steps coming up the bamboo ladder. The steps came nearer, then I saw a pair of square-toed shoes on the mat where I was lying. I felt my brother's hand on my hand, rubbing it gently.

"You will be well tomorrow," he said. "We will go to the grassy bank of the river and snare birds. Don't you want to see the white bird with the long brown legs?"

A week later Silvestre and I went to the river with snares. I don't remember whether or not I was well, but I went with him to the grassy banks. We planted several snares under the tall reeds, near the small streams that flowed into the river. We sat under the mango tree and waited, throwing pebbles into the brook where a yellow fish came up now and then for air. Late in the afternoon we looked for our snares; we had caught several birds. That evening I played with the tall bird with the brown legs under the wooden bench in our house. The bird was tied to the leg of the bench and I fed him corn. But I don't remember my brother going away—I remember only that I got well after that day. When he was gone I went to the river again and snared more birds.

Years later I knew why my brother used to go to the fields and rivers with his snares. He wanted to be alone. The life into which he was born was too small for him. That was why he went away from our family, from our town, and from the small people who lived in that little town.

When he was nineteen he returned. He was ill and wanted to go away to some quiet place. So we went back to the village where he was born. We farmed there, growing tobacco and camotes [sweet potatoes]. Sometimes we worked at night under the moonlight.

We stayed in that village one year. The crop was good, but at the beginning of the second year my brother became restless. He went to Baguio and worked for a trucking company in that city. One year later he returned to our town. He entered politics there and at twenty-four was elected vice-mayor. Before he died he erected a modern presidencia (town hall).

He died when I was in the county hospital. When I received a letter from my cousin telling me that my brother Silvestre was dead, I went to the bathroom and cried. I did not cry for him only but for all the things he could have done for his country. He was always planning, wanting to do something helpful and good for others. Like the rest of our family, he had very little formal schooling, but toward the end of his life he could read and write several languages.

I remember him for his passion to change a great many things in the town. If he were living I know he could do something toward the liberation of the Philippines. He had always rejected the narrowness of the world into which he was born. But he is dead and the country he loved is under Japan.

Now I will tell you about my brother Aurelio. He and I have known each other for a long time, especially in America, where we have lived together and shared our hopes and joys. It took a long while for us to arrive at a definite understanding, but once we had it life became simpler and the indignities that we suffered were more bearable.

My earliest memory of him is a day when I was five or six. I was alone that morning. I fell from the bamboo ladder of our house and my head was bruised very badly. When Aurelio came home from school he promised to take me to school the next day if I stopped crying.

That was how I started going to school with him. I used to walk on the dirt road to the bamboo school house, carrying his books, and sat with him on the rough bench at school. I went to school with him for three weeks, then my father came to the village and took me back to the farm.

For a long time I did not see my brother. As I grew up on the farm I began to forget him. After several years I went to town again to live with my mother, and I saw Aurelio when he came home on vacations from the capital of the province where he was attending high school. After he graduated he taught grade school in our town.

During this period (I was ten or eleven) I started working with my mother. She and I used to go to the village and barter with the natives. Once in a while we would go to the nearest town and sell the goods we bartered in the villages. We always made a little profit. And this is how my mother and I supported ourselves for several years.

We were no longer a family unit. My brother Dionisio had gone to America and we had not heard from him. And my brother Silvestre had joined the Philippine Army.

When Aurelio went to the United States several years later I thought I would lose him completely. I began to feel that my future was in America. I went away from our town and worked in several towns, learning the dialects of the people. Then I decided to go to America.

Two years after I landed in Seattle I stopped in Santa Barbara to see Aurelio. I had been traveling around on freight trains and I was tired. I needed a rest. At that time Aurelio was attending college in Santa Barbara and working at nights. He asked me if I wanted to work; he knew of a job (menial work) in a hospital. I went to work at the hospital the day after I arrived in Santa Barbara and was given a small room at the back of the building. When I had worked for several days I felt restless again. I had been on the road for almost ten months and I felt imprisoned in that little room. I left my job and for a long time I did not see Aurelio.

I traveled up and down the Pacific Coast for another year and then I decided to find work in Southern California. From that time on we lived in Los Angeles and seldom parted, except when I went out of town. But I always came back to Los Angeles, and my brother was always there.

I think Aurelio is the most human of my brothers. As the years passed he knew that it was impossible to go on with his ambitions. *He gave up everything and tried to help me.*

We used to sit up at night and talk until dawn. We talked about the problems of the Philippines and what we could do for our people in the United States. We started a movement for the protection of the civil rights of Filipinos in the United States. Aurelio spent his time and money but in the end the movement degenerated. He worked hard so that I would have leisure to read books, but for many years I felt lost and defeated.

I do not know why it is not easy to write about Aurelio. It may be because we have been so close to each other.

Have I ever told you about my brother Dionisio? He is the fourth brother, and was very close to me when we were young. I used to box with him in our yard in town, under the tall tamarind tree. But I shall begin with my most vivid memory of him.

We were in the village and Dionisio was plowing. It was raining hard. I was following him with a bamboo harrow. He was using the old carabao, but the animal became exhausted and stopped in the middle of the field. It was late and Dionisio wanted to finish the plowing. He became impatient and angry. He beat the animal ferociously with a long stick, but it would not go on. Slumped in the mud, it paid no attention to his frantic abuse. My father, who was watching us from a small hill nearby where he was bundling stalks of rice, came running.

"You shouldn't beat the animal!" Father yelled.

He slapped Dionisio across the face and Dionisio turned around and looked at me as if seeking my assistance. I thought it best not to say anything. Without a word, Dionisio flung down the rope that was attached to the carabao and the plow and went toward the house.

I never saw him again in the Philippines. He went to the grass house, gathered his clothes, and walked to town. From the town he went to Manila and after a year he sailed to America. I did not see him for seven years.

One night in San Francisco I was eating a sandwich at the counter of a restaurant on Kearny Street. It was dimly lighted and I could not see the people around me. Suddenly the man next to me said, "Just got in?"

"Yes," I said. I looked up and saw the familiar face of my brother.

For a moment he stared at me dubiously and then he was no longer in doubt. He put his arm around my shoulders and squeezed my arm. He wanted to say something emotional but changed his mind.

"I didn't know you came to America."

"I arrived ten months ago," I said.

He touched my hands. He was still the same boy I used to plow with back there in the buried village of my childhood.

"Let's get away from here," he said.

We left and walked the foggy streets. There were many people on the streets because this was at the height of the depression. I had just got into town on one of the freight trains from Seattle. My brother knew that I had been riding the freights.

He took me to a little bar, and we sat at a table near the rear. We drank beer for a couple of hours and talked over much that had happened to us during the time since he had left the Philippines. When we tired of sitting there we went to a dance hall and watched the Filipinos with their girls. Toward dawn we went to his room somewhere in Chinatown.

In the morning he took me to breakfast. When we had finished eating he handed me fifteen dollars in bills.

"Take this," he said.

I did not want to because he was not working.

"Take it," he insisted. "I'll find work in the morning."

I took his money and went away again. I did not see him for several months, and then we would meet casually but unexpectedly. Sometimes I would see him in some town drinking at a bar, sometimes I would find him in dirty dance halls. But he was always kind and cheerful. Whenever I needed him he was there with his money.

I began to understand my brother. He hated money as much as he hated his childhood. When we were together he would start talking about the years of his youth. I knew that his childhood pained him, as it pained me, and he lacked a certain system of thought to guide him in his rootlessness.

I remember the time I received the advance copies of my first book here in L.A. I went to his hotel room to show him that at last I had done something for myself in America. He was not in his room so I went downstairs and looked for him at the bar. Toward midnight I found him in a restaurant on Temple Street.

He was with several persons, strangers to me. Many times I tried to tell him that I was giving him a copy of my book. When I finally managed to mention the subject one of the girls became foolishly maudlin. "Book?" she asked tearfully. "Did *you* write a book?" Then she accidentally spilled beer on the book.

My brother slapped the girl across the face.

"Don't do that!" he shouted.

I got up from the table and walked toward the door. I glanced back once at my brother. Then I knew that his seeming dislike of intellectual things was only an armor against dull surroundings. I walked into the night holding the book close, for now it was not merely a book to me: it was the youth of my brother Dionisio, the young boy who ran away one day when were were plowing. It was my brother at last, the real boy that I knew back there in the village. I walked for miles, and the light mist that covered the city that night was like the rays of the morning sun.

Carlos

July 2, 1942

Dear D.,

I am writing his letter after I finished packing. I wanted to say more than I did this afternoon when we parted, but I had no time to say anything except to skim over irrelevant matters. However, I will remember that last moment.

I am not going away this evening, maybe I'll go Saturday evening. A few things have been delayed and I must stay here for several days. I have tried to arrange my affairs before I go because I may not come to Los Angeles again. I have been going around for the last few months in a kind of desperation, but I am all right now.

In spite of everything that has happened to me in America I am not sorry that I was born a Filipino. When I say "Filipino" the sound cuts deep into my being—it hurts.

All these years you were prominent in my mind. I think there was not a day that I did not think of you with tenderness. Everything fine and gentle that came into my life since I met you was associated with your gentleness and fine ways. There were times when I cried, knowing that you were gone and lost, knowing that I had nobody to talk to with a certain feeling of equality.

One of these days you will sit down and recall everything I have said. You will recall everything and know that I have been good.

I will never forget you: never. I will never forget what you have given me.

I have thought of you in a wonderful way, so please don't destroy my wonderful memory of you. Wherever I go with my Filipino friends or with my Filipino intellectual acquaintances I speak of you highly and with sincerity.

I have nothing against the world now. I don't even hate white America any more. What is the use hating?

I think you will understand that I have said everything here. I have very little time left in the world and I should like it to be memorable and beautiful.

I hope you are happy. As for myself, I don't care if I am happy or not.

I am proud that I am a Filipino. I used to be angry, to question myself. But now I am proud.

And so good-bye.

Carlos

Letter to a Filipino Woman

Dear Mrs. Lopez:

I was informed that when your husband was murdered by the Japanese you fled to the mountains and continued his gallant work. It seems so long since I met you and your husband in Los Angeles, when you were on your way to New York to attend the American Writers' Congress. And I lost touch with you when you went to Europe; then again when you returned to the Philippines.

That was a long journey for both of you, from the Philippines to America and then to Europe. Hitler was about ready to start his monstrous war against humanity. But it gave S. P.,* as we used to call your husband, a clearer perspective of our country and a deeper understanding of our history. As we all know, he came from the peasantry. It was for the peasants that he wrote exuberantly because he, above all other writers in the Philippines, understood the function of literature in the building of society. He wanted to record and interpret our hopes as a people, desiring the fullest fulfilment of our native genius. He spoke with a strong voice, objective in criticism, protest and challenge, because it was the most effective way to combat any abortive decadence in our culture.

S. P. could have escaped death, but he heroically kept to his task. He knew beyond any shadow of a doubt that this is a war of survival. He had a wonderful dream for our people; he also had a strong hold on our history. He showed it to us in his magnificent, lyrical book, "Literature and Society."

When I think of the cruelty of the Japanese, I cannot help thinking of

---

*Salvador P. Lopez, who was the most important Filipino writer in English, continued, after the fall of Bataan and Corregidor, to inspire resistance against Japan through a hidden radio station, "The Voice of Freedom." He was murdered along with several others, which was actually the beginning of the ruthless reprisal against Filipino intellectuals.—C. B. [Lopez survived the war and became a distinguished statesman of the Republic of the Philippines.—Ed.]

your frail, childlike body, hiding in dangerous mountains, at the mercy of privation and dreaded diseases. It has fallen upon you to inspire continued resistance against the enemy, and to fight equally on all three fronts in order to vanquish him completely. First, you are resisting aggression with everything that our people can use; second, you are winning backward elements over to the camp of resistance; third, you are annihilating all that is corrupt and rotten in our national life. These are the fundamentals of your husband's broad vision of our native land; but they are also the realities that he wanted us to grasp in full.

It was S. P. who first achieved the needed articulation of social ideas in the Philippines. He had hopes that our culture would bloom as it should in our time. We were nearing what would have been the most significant achievement of our generation when Japan invaded our country and destroyed our freedom. We would have been able to focus our virginal talents on a new vista of literature, that is, to speak to the Filipino masses and to be understood by them.

Yes, S. P. is not dead to us who have searched for the mainsprings of our great tradition in the welter of imported middle-class ideals and illusions. He who had discovered the origins of our love for freedom, who had interpreted our history in terms of liberty, will live immortally with us like José Rizal, who gave us the finest seed of our culture. Some of us, even among our own people, would have learned to hate S. P. for the brave democratic ideas that he advocated; but he knew that history is on our side, and fascism is the antagonist of culture and civilization.

This is the greatest responsibility of literature in our time: to find in our national struggle that which has a future. Literature is a growing and living thing. We must destroy that which is dying, because it does not die by itself. We must interpret the resistance against the enemy by linking it with the stirring political awakening of the people and those liberating progressive forces that call for a complete social consciousness.

As I write this sentence, I hear that a soldier is being decorated for bravery. Your husband was also a hero, but his heroism is of a different nature. It is a heroism of the spirit: a heroism of building a new society. I can understand his heroism because I live in a country which is, like the Philippines, fighting courageously on many fronts in order that the shackled forces of industry will flow for all. We are engaged in the gigantic task of building a new America. Whatever we are doing, we are all working toward a democratic society.

We in America understand the many imperfections of democracy and the malignant disease which has been corroding its very heart. That is why in this war we are bringing into the light our real aims and purposes. We are united in the effort to make an America in which the common man can find happiness. It has been his unhappy lot to suffer the injustices of a system that suppresses his aspirations for a better life.

It is this feeling for democracy that binds me to the memory of your husband. I remember his poignant remark when I told you before you left that for a long time I was illiterate and miserable in America. He said: "It is a great wrong that anyone in America, whether he be white or brown, should be illiterate or hungry or miserable." The story of my struggle toward clarity of thinking and living is symptomatic of the revolutionary march of the people toward a better life.

I wanted to live in an America where there is freedom for all regardless of color, station and beliefs. This deep conviction had led me to study the lives of the great Americans; from their examples I found what they wanted to do for this continent. They worked with unselfish devotion toward one goal, that is, to use the power of the myriad peoples in the service of America's freedom. They made it their guiding principle. In this we are the same, because even before the war you fought for a Philippines where a man should be given unconditional opportunities to cultivate his potentialities and restore him to his rightful dignity.

It is but fair to say that America is not a land of one race or one class of men. We are all America that have toiled and suffered and known oppression and defeat, from the first Indian that died in Manhattan to the last Filipino that bled to death in the foxholes of Bataan. America is not bound by geographical latitudes. America is not merely a land or an institution. America is in the hearts of men that died for freedom; it is also in the eyes of men that are building a new world. America is the prophecy of a new society of men: of a system that knows no sorrow or strife or suffering. America is a warning to those who would try to falsify the ideals of free men.

America is also the nameless foreigner, the homeless refugee, the hungry boy begging for a job and the black body dangling from a tree. America is the illiterate immigrant who is ashamed that the world of books and intellectual opportunities is closed to him. We are all that nameless foreigner, that homeless refugee, that hungry boy, that illiterate immigrant and that lynched black body. All of us, from the first Adams to the last Bulosan, native born or alien, educated or illiterate— *We are America!*

Now America is in mortal danger, within and without, from selfishness and greed, from the terror of the powerful who want more power, and from the unenlightened who fear new ideas. Like you and those who defended Bataan, we in America will refuse all offers of appeasement or compromise. No price is too high to pay for freedom; those who lack the courage to pay for it have no place in America. He who has not the courage to choose death instead of slavery is not a free man.

We will stand by America always, and renew the grand epic of democracy that *was* hers. We will interpret her in a language relevant to the understanding and the living of the common man, by using only the words and thinking the thoughts that he is desperately trying to reach. The common man is intuitively seeking the secret of fighting the war, because he is intuitively seeking the secret of fighting the peace. He is awakening to the necessity of a central democratic consciousness of universal freedom.

So, whether you are in the Philippines or in the United States, you are a part of the growing consciousness of universal freedom. When Japan attacked Manila and Pearl Harbor, and American writers stirred the democratic conscience of the world, we were all passing through a heroic conflict not unlike the heroism through which your husband passed through to death. I can understand why S. P. stood his ground. He had no sympathy for those who tried to annihilate our people's freedom with their philosophy of darkness.

S. P. wanted to abolish tenantry in our country; it was the blight of our national life. He advocated universal education, cultural revival, literary revaluations, popularization of folklore, rediscovery of our history, alliances with writers in other countries, and discussed these things in a language pertinent to our national struggle for liberty. But the terror of Japanese imperialism is let loose in the world, and you in the Philippines and we in America have a common enemy.

We who are free will supply the human inspiration to resist aggression to the end. I know that out of this struggle will come a new race of men, and history will flow forward again.

The old world is dying, but a new world is being born. It generates inspiration from the chaos that beats upon us all. The false grandeur and security, the unfulfilled promises and illusory power, the number of the dead and those who are about to die, will charge the forces of our courage and determination. The old world will die so that the new world will be born with less sacrifice and agony for the living. . . .

This is all that I can say about him who was your dear husband and my good friend.

Carlos Bulosan

Autobiographical Sketch

BULOSAN, CARLOS (November 24, 1914–), Filipino poet and memorist, writes: "I was born in a small village in the Philippines. The province is Pangasinan, the town is Binalonan, and the village is Mangusmana. When I was born Mangusmana was still a wilderness; the great forest on the eastern slope of the village teemed with wild game, and the mountains to the north were untrodden by man. On the south were the wide fertile plains of Luzon, extending as far as Manila, the capital of the Philippines; while on the west were rivers, crisscrossing growing towns and expanding sugarcane plantations until they met the China Sea. I started working when I was five.

"Today the village of Mangusmana is nearly gone, eaten away by the Tagamusin River, a tributary of the Agno River which flows to Lingayen Gulf. I lived in Mangusmana with my father until I was seven years old. We lived in a small grass hut; but it was sufficient, because we were peasants. My father could not read or write, but he knew how to work his one hectare of land, which was the sole support of our big family.

"The rest of the family lived in a palm-leaf house in Binalonan. It consisted of four brothers and two sisters. Here my mother was the driving force, who sold salted fish in the public market to feed and clothe her children. Being the youngest of the five brothers, I was obligated to help my mother in the house and in the marketplace. My mother could not read or write; but she was such a dynamic little peasant woman that, when her sons had all grown up and were scattered in many lands, she gathered the numerous grandchildren in her fold and raised them alone as she had done to her own children. Today, at the age of eighty, she is still supporting her last five grandchildren by selling salted fish in the public market of Binalonan.

"Off and on I went to the public school of Binalonan until I was thirteen, then to the high school in Lingayen, where I stayed for three semesters. Then I quit school forever and went to work in Baguio, the summer capital of the Philippines. Later I returned to Binalonan and worked on the farm until I came to the United States in 1931.

"The next period of my life is recorded in my autobiography, *America Is in the Heart*. Between 1931 and Pearl Harbor day, I lived violent years of unemployment, prolonged illnesses, and heart-rending labor union work on the farms of California. It was when I was dying of tuberculosis in the Los Angeles County Hospital that I had the opportunity to seriously read books which opened all my world of intellectual possibilities—and a grand dream of bettering society for the working man.

"I stayed in this hospital two years. But it took me another five years before I was able to put my grand dream on paper in a literate form. When it began—my relentless creative activity began. And many things followed from my typewriter for two restless years—poetry, short stories, articles on political and cultural subjects. And books—*The Laughter of My Father* (written in twelve days), *The Voice of Bataan* (three days), *America Is in the Heart* (twenty-four days), *Chorus for America, Letter from America*, and two books for children, as well as *The Dark People*.

"Today I have published poetry, short stories, and serious articles in many magazines—enough to fill three more books.

"I am sick again. I know I will be here (Firland Sanitarium, Seattle, Wash.) for a long time. And the grass hut where I was born is gone, and the village of Mangusmana is gone, and my father and his one hectare of land are gone, too. And the palm-leaf house in Binalonan is gone, and two brothers and a sister are gone forever.

"But what does it matter to me? The question is—what impelled me to write? The answer is—my grand dream of equality among men and freedom for all. To give a literate voice to the voiceless one hundred thousand Filipinos in the United States, Hawaii, and Alaska. Above all and ultimately, to translate the desires and aspirations of the whole Filipino people in the Philippines and abroad in terms relevant to contemporary history.

"Yes, I have taken unto myself this sole responsibility."

Selected Writings by and about Carlos Bulosan

Anthologies

Bulosan: An Introduction with Selections. Edited by E. San Juan, Jr. Manila: National Book Store, 1983.

If You Want to Know What We Are. Edited by E. San Juan, Jr. Albuquerque, NM: West End Press, 1983.

Selected Works and Letters. Edited E. San Juan, Jr., and Ninotchka Rosca. Honolulu: Friends of the Filipino People, 1982. Includes hitherto unpublished letters to Dorothy Babb.

Writings of Carlos Bulosan. Edited by E. San Juan, Jr. Special issue of *Amerasia Journal* 6:1 (May 1979). Includes a substantial bibliography of Bulosan's published works.

Fiction

America Is in the Heart. New York: Harcourt, Brace and Co., 1946. Reprint. Seattle: University of Washington Press, 1973.

"As Long As the Grass Shall Grow." *Common Ground* 9:4 (Summer 1949): 38–43.

The Cry and the Dedication. Edited by E. San Juan, Jr. Philadelphia: Temple University Press, 1995.

"The End of the War." *New Yorker,* September 2, 1944, pp. 21–23.

The Laughter of My Father. New York: Harcourt, Brace and Co., 1944.

The Philippines Is in the Heart. Edited by E. San Juan, Jr. Quezon City: New Day Publishers, 1978.

The Power of Money and Other Stories. Manila: Kalikasan Press, 1990.

The Power of the People. Special issue of *Alive Magazine* 10 (September 1977). Reprint. Manila: National Book Store, 1986; with an introduction by E. San Juan, Jr.

Nonfiction

"Editorial." In *1952 Yearbook, ILWU Local 37,* p. 4. Seattle: International Longshoreman's and Warehouseman's Union, 1952.

"Filipino Writers in a Changing World." *Books Abroad* 16 (Summer 1942): 252–53.

"Freedom from Want." *Saturday Evening Post,* March 6, 1943.

"The Growth of Philippine Culture." *The Teacher's Journal* 5 (May–June 1951): 1–10.

"I Am Not a Laughing Man." *The Writer* 59 (May 1946): 143–45.

"Letter to a Filipino Woman." *The New Republic,* November 8, 1943, pp. 645–46.

"Man against the World." *Commonwealth Times,* August 28, 1940, pp. 8–9.

"Manuel L. Quezon–The Good Fight!" *Bataan Magazine,* August 1944, pp. 13–15.

Sound of Falling Light: Letters in Exile. Edited by Dolores Feria. Quezon City: University of the Philippines Press, 1960. Also in *Diliman Review,* January–September 1960, pp. 185–278.

"The Writer As Worker." *Midweek,* July 27, 1988, pp. 30–31.

"To Whom it May Concern." In *1952 Yearbook, ILWU Local 37,* p. 21. Seattle: International Longshoreman's and Warehouseman's Union, 1952.

Poetry

Carlos Bulosan and His Poetry. Edited by Susan Evangelista. Quezon City: Ateneo de Manila University Press, 1985.

Chorus for America: Six Filipino Poets. Edited by Carlos Bulosan. Los Angeles: Wagon and Star, 1942.

"If You Want to Know What We Are." In *Literature under the Commonwealth,* edited by Manuel Arguilla et al., pp. 48–50. Manila: Philippine Writers League, 1940.

Letter from America. Prairie City, IL: J. A. Decker, 1942.

The Voice of Bataan. New York: Coward-McCann, 1943.

Criticism and Commentary on Bulosan

Alquizola, Marilyn. "The Fictive Narrator of *America Is in the Heart*." In *Frontiers in Asian American Studies*, edited by Gail Nomura et al., pp. 211–17. Pullman: Washington State University Press, 1989.

———. "Subversion or Affirmation: The Text and Subtext of *America Is in the Heart*." In *Asian Americans: Comparative and Global Perspectives*, edited by Shirley Hune et al., pp. 199–209. Pullman: Washington State University Press, 1991.

Campomanes, Oscar. "Filipinos in the United States and Their Literature of Exile." In *Reading the Literatures of Asian America*, edited by Shirley Geok-lin Lim and Amy Ling, pp. 49–78. Philadelphia: Temple University Press, 1992.

———, and Todd Gernes. "Two Letters from America: Carlos Bulosan and the Act of Writing." *MELUS* 15:3 (Fall 1988): 15–46.

Daroy, Petronilo. "Carlos Bulosan: The Politics of Literature." *Saint Louis Quarterly* 6:2 (June 1968): 193–206.

Evangelista, Susan. *Carlos Bulosan and His Poetry*. Quezon City: Ateneo de Manila University Press, 1985.

Feria, Dolores. "Carlos Bulosan: Gentle Genius." *Comment* 1 (1957): 57–64.

Kim, Elaine. *Asian American Literature: An Introduction to the Writings and Their Social Context*. Philadelphia: Temple University Press, 1982.

San Juan, Jr., E. "Carlos Bulosan." In *The American Radical*, edited by Mari Jo Buhle, Paul Buhle, and Harvey Kaye, pp. 253–60. New York: Routledge, 1994.

———. "Carlos Bulosan: The Poetics and Necessity of Revolution." *The Researcher* 2 (1969): 113–23.

———. *Carlos Bulosan and the Imagination of the Class Struggle*. Quezon City: University of the Philippines Press, 1972.

———. "Filipino Writing in the United States: Reclaiming Whose America?" *Philippine Studies* 41 (1993): 141–66. A longer version will appear in *Revising the Ethnic Canon*, edited by David Palumbo-Liu. Minneapolis: University of Minnesota Press, 1995.

———. *Reading the West/Writing the East*. New York: Peter Lang, 1993.

Tolentino, Delfin. "Satire in Carlos Bulosan's *The Laughter of My Father*." *Philippine Studies* 34 (1986): 452–61.

Wong, Sau-ling Cynthia. *Reading Asian American Literature: From Necessity to Extravagance*. Princeton: Princeton University Press, 1993.

About the Editor

E. San Juan, Jr., professor of English and Comparative Literature at the University of Connecticut, received his graduate degrees from the University of the Philippines and Harvard University. He has taught at the University of California and Brooklyn College, City University of New York. He was the 1987–88 Fulbright Lecturer in the Philippines and a 1993 Fellow at the Institute of Humanities, University of Edinburgh.

San Juan's recent works are *Reading the West/Writing the East* and *Racial Formations/Critical Transformations;* the latter received the National Book Award from the Association for Asian American Studies and an Outstanding Book Award from the Gustavus Myers Center for Human Rights. His collection of short fiction, *The Smile of the Medusa,* was published by Anvil Press in Manila, Philippines, this year. Temple University Press will release three books by San Juan in 1995: two editions of Carlos Bulosan's writings, *On Becoming Filipino* and *The Cry and the Dedication;* and a collection of critical essays, *The Philippine Temptation.* Two other books are scheduled for release soon: *Hegemony and Strategies of Transgression: Essays in Cultural Studies and Comparative Literature* and *Allegories of Resistance.*

San Juan is on the editorial board of *The Arkansas Review* and *Nature, Society and Thought.* He is also a Scientific Board member of the Institute for Critical Research (Amsterdam, the Netherlands) and a member of the National Association of Ethnic Scholars and the International Gramsci Society. He is currently directing Seminars in Ethnic Studies and American Culture at Bowling Green State University, Ohio.